Understanding and Loving Your Child
with ADHD

UNDERSTANDING AND LOVING YOUR CHILD

WITH

STEPHEN ARTERBURN
AND MICHAEL ROSS

SALEM
BOOKS
an imprint of Regnery Publishing
Washington, D.C.

Scriptures marked CEV are taken from the CONTEMPORARY ENG-
LISH VERSION. Copyright © 1995 by the American Bible Society. Used by
permission.
Scriptures marked NIV are taken from THE HOLY BIBLE, NEW INTER-
NATIONAL VERSION.® Copyright © 1973, 1978, 1984, 2011 by Biblica,
Inc.™ Used by permission of Zondervan.
Scriptures marked NIRV are taken from the NEW INTERNATIONAL
READER'S VERSION. Copyright © 1995, 1996, 1998, 2014 by Biblica,
Inc.® Used by permission. All rights reserved worldwide.

Salem Books™ is a trademark of Salem Communications Holding
Corporation
Regnery® is a registered trademark and its colophon is a trademark of
Salem Communications Holding Corporation

Cataloging-in-Publication data on file with the Library of Congress

ISBN: 978-1-68451-153-2
eISBN: 978-1-68451-203-4

Library of Congress Control Number: 2021936543

Published in the United States by
Salem Books
An Imprint of Regnery Publishing
A Division of Salem Media Group
Washington, D.C.
www.SalemBooks.com

Manufactured in the United States of America

10 9 8 7 6 5 4 3 2 1

Books are available in quantity for promotional or premium use. For information on discounts and terms, please visit our website: www.SalemBooks.com.

CONTENTS

PART ONE

UNDERSTANDING ADHD

CHAPTER 1

Recognizing the Signs and Symptoms

Is It Time to See the Doctor? Take Our Quiz and Find Out

As early as first grade, Sondra's boy Ethan struggled in social settings—usually at school, but also at church and during playdates with friends. He was constantly moving and squirming, interrupting kids and adults, and rarely listening or following rules.

"Ethan, slow down!" became just about every adult's mantra, followed by, "I need you to stop what you're doing, put your arms down, look me in the eye...and listen!"

By second grade, Ethan's teacher had devised a "behavior chart" that tracked disciplinary issues, including inattentive behaviors. She then emailed weekly updates to Sondra—along with a rundown on how Ethan had "missed the mark" in her class: "Each day, Ethan had trouble focusing, he would often cut lines, and he wouldn't share with other children. We had to place him in time-out six times in three days!"

Sondra couldn't help groaning as she read each note. The teacher's smiley-face, frowny-face charts felt so demeaning to her. This just isn't working, Sondra thought. Yes, my kid is downright ornery at times. Yet to constantly tell him "no" or to "stop" and then to put him in time-out and label him with a frowny face has got to be crushing what little self-esteem he has left.

Ethan really was a good kid—so sweet, so loveable. He deserved better. Yet Sondra had no idea how to distinguish "common kid behaviors" from the possible signs of something more serious that could be going on.

Thankfully, a much-needed helping hand came through Ethan's third-grade teacher, who concluded that Ethan was simply unable to control his inattentive behaviors on his own, and agreed that behavior charts were making things worse. "I think Ethan's issue is medical," he told Sondra, "and it very well could be a neurodevelopmental disorder such as ADHD. So, with your permission, I'd like for a school psychologist to spend a day observing your son. She'll be able to give us some clues on what might be driving Ethan's behavior."

Sondra wholeheartedly agreed, and within twenty-four hours, she had a recommendation: Get Ethan evaluated for ADHD. One week later, she sat with him in the exam room of Ethan's pediatrician, who conducted a full physical and bloodwork, not to mention a preliminary evaluation of Ethan's emotional well-being.

"Overall, he's a healthy kid," the doctor told Sondra. "Results from the bloodwork will tell us more. But at this point, I'm going to refer you to a psychiatrist who can make a diagnosis as well. All the signs are leaning toward ADHD."

Soon, Sondra had an official diagnosis: Ethan did in fact have ADHD-Inattentive Type. This meant school administrators could write up a 504 Plan for the boy, and they could finally get him the help he needed at school.[1]

Sondra was relieved. Though it wasn't easy for her to accept that there was something atypical about her child, "I've come to accept the fact that my kid, like all children, is imperfect," she later told one of her closest girlfriends. "I'm learning that ADHD in children is common but not straightforward. So we're going to make the best of this, and I'm going to see that Ethan gets the best education and the best future possible."

But as the weeks turned into months, Sondra's frustrations began to grow again, and Ethan continued to fall behind at school—and get into trouble with his teacher.

"I'm so sorry to report this," the teacher told Sondra at the classroom door, "but we had a rough day today. Ethan just wouldn't stay focused."

"Did you check his backpack?" Sondra asked. "We have a 504 Plan with instructions in the backpack—"

"No," the teacher interrupted. "I didn't check it, and I'm sorry. I have twenty-four other children and one assistant, so I overlooked it."

Sondra took a deep breath, and then spoke. "I get it, you're busy," she said. "But if you could just read the instructions, you'll find that they are so clear...and they really will make a difference for Ethan—and you. It's all a part of the plan, and it will work if we can follow it."

Six months later, Sondra was having the same conversations with Ethan's teacher, who simply did not have the time or energy to follow a state-issued 504 Plan. Meanwhile, Sondra put Ethan on a strict no-sugar diet but soon discovered it wasn't helping, either.

"All this hard work trying to normalize life for my son, and yet it feels as if it's falling apart," Sondra told her friend. "We've really taken this seriously, checking Ethan's backpack every night for notes from his teacher, talking to him about interactions at school, and having him repeat back to me directions for his homework. But he's still not improving, so I think it's time to take the next step..."

After more than eight months and no success using the 504 Plan, Sondra decided to put Ethan on ADHD medication.

She and his doctor agreed to a low dose of the stimulant Adderall—just to see how Ethan would react. Four weeks later, Ethan's teacher sent home a positive report: "Ethan is participating more, as well as giving me his full attention and showing more interest in the assignments I hand out."

Medication wasn't Sondra's first choice for her son, but it was working. And the balance that was finally achieved in her eight-year-old's life allowed Sondra and her husband to enjoy a long-overdue date night.

For years, she and her husband worried that a sitter wouldn't be equipped to handle their son's special needs. They tried hiring a teenager, but it didn't work out, and the experience left them even more nervous—so the couple just didn't get out much. But as Ethan gradually began to improve, the couple felt comfortable leaving their boy with a sitter.

An actual couple's night out, and coming home to a peaceful house, Sondra thought, that's every parent's dream; a dream I'm ready to live!

■ ■ ■

Can you relate to this young mother's dilemma with her boy? Do you suspect that your own child has ADHD, but—like Sondra—you aren't sure how to distinguish "common kid behaviors" from the possible signs of a neurodevelopmental disorder?

Two of the most frequently asked questions we receive from parents are "What are the signs and symptoms of ADHD?" and "How can I sort them out from normal kid stuff?"

At some point, nearly every child gets fidgety in church, tunes out a teacher, blocks simple instructions, or acts impulsively around friends. And what kid doesn't have an occasional meltdown or refuse to share or take turns? It's all par for the course in most healthy households. Here's the difference with ADHD—a red flag that could mean it's time to see a medical professional: ADHD may be present in your child if you observe a persistent pattern of inattention and/or hyperactivity-impulsivity that interferes with functioning or development.[2]

If the signs are few and far between, and if you notice them only in certain situations—such as with a specific group of kids or only in the classroom—then your child probably does not have a neurodevelopmental disorder. On the other hand, if he or she shows several symptoms that are present across all situations—at home, at school, and at play—it's time to take a closer look.[3]

Ready to get started? Let's begin with a quiz. Don't worry, it's one that we guarantee you'll pass! (But we can't promise that you'll like the results.) While the intention here isn't to provide a scientific evaluation of your child—or to provide an official diagnosis—the goal is to help you gain insight into your kid's behavior. Are you observing a persistent pattern of inattention and/or hyperactivity-impulsivity? Are six or more of the symptoms persisting for six months or longer? Is your child developing socially or academically at a pace that's consistent with other kids their age?

The quiz below will help you assess where your child is right now. You'll get a snapshot of not only observable patterns, but also to what extent they are affecting your child's life. If much of your child's world is severely impacted by inattention and/or hyperactivity-impulsivity, it's a good idea to get a thorough examination from your family doctor.

Please read each question and think about how often each statement has been true of your child in the past month.

ASSESSING YOUR CHILD FOR ADHD

	Never	Sometimes	Often	Always
My child seems self-focused and unable to recognize other people's needs and desires.	0	1	2	3

	Never	Sometimes	Often	Always
My child constantly interrupts me, other adults (such as teachers), and even kids.	0	1	2	3
My child struggles with taking turns.	0	1	2	3
My child can't keep his/her emotions in check.	0	1	2	3
My child simply can't sit still and seems to fidget constantly.	0	1	2	3
My child has trouble paying attention—at home, in the classroom, and with the team.	0	1	2	3
My child struggles to play quietly.	0	1	2	3
My child avoids activities that require sustained mental effort, such as paying attention in class or completing homework assignments.	0	1	2	3
My child makes careless mistakes on tasks because he/she has trouble following instructions that require planning.	0	1	2	3

	Never	Sometimes	Often	Always
My child can't get organized or keep track of tasks and activities.	0	1	2	3
My child seems quieter than other kids, often staring into space and daydreaming.	0	1	2	3
My child is forgetful and often loses things such as toys.	0	1	2	3
Add the numbers you circled in each column.				

Now add the total for each column to get your score: _____

What Does Your Score Mean?

If your score is twelve or less, it is *unlikely* that your child is struggling with ADHD. While your son or daughter may become fidgety or forgetful or act impulsively on occasion, you haven't observed consistent patterns of inattention and/or hyperactivity-impulsivity. But keep reading. This book is all about helping you to understand and love your child—whether or not ADHD is an issue—and it's packed full of tips and ideas that can help you strengthen the parent-child connection. What's more, it doesn't hurt to seek a medical assessment just to be sure.

If your score is more than thirteen but less than twenty-one, it is *possible* that your child is struggling with ADHD. Although it may not always hold them back, your son or daughter may experience difficulty focusing on tasks, and he or she may struggle to concentrate on school assignments. You may also observe impulsivity and hyperactivity. It's important that you study the strategies outlined in this book, especially Chapters 2, 3, and 8, and that you seek a medical assessment.

If your score is more than twenty-one, it is *probable* that your child is struggling with ADHD. In order for your child to be diagnosed with ADHD, he or she must have at least six or more of the following symptoms: (1) a lack of attention to details/makes careless mistakes; (2) difficulty sustaining attention; (3) doesn't listen when spoken to; (4) doesn't follow instructions and fails to finish schoolwork, projects, or chores; (5) difficulty organizing tasks; (6) avoids tasks that require sustained attention; (7) loses things necessary to complete a task; (8) distracted by things around them; (9) forgetful in daily activities; (10) fidgets; (11) leaves seat often for no reason; (12) constantly restless; (13) can't engage in activities quietly; (14) often on the go; (15) talks excessively; (16) blurts out answers; (17) difficulty waiting for a turn; and (18) interrupts conversations with others.

It's essential that you consult your doctor and have your child evaluated for ADHD. This book will guide you through the process—from the initial meeting with your primary health care provider to the key steps you'd be wise to follow once you receive an official diagnosis.

No single treatment is the answer for every child with ADHD. Instead, each child's needs and unique personal history must be carefully considered by a medical professional. For example, it's possible that your son or daughter may have an allergic reaction to certain medications, making a particular treatment unacceptable. And if your kid has anxiety or depression, a treatment plan that combines medication and behavioral therapy may be best. Your doctor will help you find the best solution for your child.

■ ■ ■

With your ADHD assessment complete and a general idea of what you need to focus on with your child, it's time to take the next crucial steps. We'll begin with a clear yet simple definition of ADHD, zeroing in on the symptoms of inattention and hyperactivity-impulsivity. Next, we'll explore the details medical professionals look for when they diagnose this disorder. Here's what we'll include in the mix: (1) a practical look at how ADHD affects children at different developmental stages, (2) the factors that determine the severity of ADHD, and (3) an ADHD checklist you can use as a conversation

LET'S GO DEEPER

UNDERSTANDING AND LOVING THE ADHD CHILD

In the remainder of this chapter, we will...

▶ Learn what ADHD is and what's going on in a child's brain

▶ Examine the common symptoms of ADHD

▶ Spot the signs of ADHD in loved ones

starter should you decide to meet with a health care professional.

What Is Attention-Deficit Disorder?

We've all encountered children who just can't seem sit still or listen. They blurt out inappropriate comments at inappropriate moments, they talk back to adults, they don't share or take turns, and they simply can't follow instructions—regardless of how clearly the instructions are presented. Essentially, these are the signs of attention-deficit/hyperactivity disorder (ADHD). It's a neurodevelopmental disorder that is usually first diagnosed in childhood (before age twelve) and can harm a child's relationships with peers and adults and can hinder their success in school. Here's how the American Psychiatric Association defines it: "The essential feature of attention-deficit/hyperactivity disorder (ADHD) is a persistent pattern of inattention and/or hyperactivity-impulsivity that interferes with functioning or development."[4]

Attention problems may include daydreaming, difficulty tuning in and staying focused, and the tendency to be easily distracted. Hyperactivity refers to fidgeting or restlessness. According to researchers at Harvard Medical School, children with ADHD probably have an underlying genetic vulnerability to developing it, but the severity of the problem is also influenced by their environment.[5]

ADHD makes it difficult for children to inhibit their spontaneous responses—which can involve everything from movement to speech to attentiveness. Sometimes these children are labeled as "troublemakers" or criticized for being lazy and undisciplined. However, they may have ADHD.[6]

Three Basic Types of ADHD in Children

- Hyperactive/Impulsive Type—Children show both hyperactive and impulsive behavior, but for the most part, they are able to pay attention.
- Inattentive Type—These children are not overly active. They do not disrupt the classroom or other activities, so their symptoms might not be noticed.
- Combined Type (Inattentive and Hyperactive/Impulsive)—Children with this type of ADHD

show both categories of symptoms. This is the most common form of ADHD.

Kids with hyperactivity always seem to be in motion. They can't sit still and may dash around or talk incessantly. Children with ADHD are unable to sit still and pay attention in class. They may roam around the room, squirm in their seats, wiggle their feet, touch everything, or noisily tap a pencil. Older adolescents and adults with ADHD may feel intensely restless.

Impulsivity isn't hard to spot, either. Children who are overly impulsive seem unable to think before they act. As a result, they may blurt out answers to questions, make inappropriate comments, or run into the street without looking. Their impulsivity may make it difficult for them to wait for things they want or to take their turn in games. They may grab a toy from another child or hit when they are upset. They often have difficulty making and keeping friends.

And who can miss the inattentive child? Youngsters who struggle with this symptom have a hard time keeping their mind focused on one thing and may get bored with a task after only a few minutes. Focusing conscious, deliberate attention to organizing and completing routine tasks may be difficult. Often, they lose track of things or forget things easily. You may notice restlessness, procrastination, problems remembering obligations, trouble staying seated during meetings or activities, or starting multiple projects at the same time but rarely finishing them.

Your Child May Have ADHD If...

✓ There is a persistent pattern of inattention and/or hyperactivity-impulsivity

✓ Six or more of the symptoms have persisted for six months or longer

✓ Your child isn't developing socially or academically at a pace that's consistent with other kids his/her age

Common Symptoms in Children

The definitions and descriptions we've presented here are based on what the American Psychiatric Association has published in the *Diagnostic and Statistical Manual of Mental Disorders*, Fifth Edition (DSM-5), its guide for therapists and medical professionals.[7]

The symptoms of ADHD—inattention, hyperactivity, or impulsive behavior—often show up first at school. A teacher may report to parents that their child won't listen, is "hyper," or causes trouble and is disruptive. A child with ADHD often wants to be a good student, but the symptoms get in the way. Teachers, parents, and friends may be unsympathetic because they see the child's behavior as bad or odd.[8]

A high level of activity and occasional impulsiveness or inattentiveness is often normal in a child. But the hyperactivity of ADHD is typically more haphazard, poorly organized, and has no real purpose. And in children with ADHD, these behaviors are frequent enough that the child has a harder than average time learning, getting along with others, or staying reasonably safe.

ADHD symptoms can vary widely. Here are common characteristics of the disorder in the two major groups (inattention and hyperactivity).

Inattention

Carelessness: Fails to give close attention to details or makes careless mistakes in schoolwork, at work, or during other activities. For example, overlooks or misses details, work is inaccurate.

Difficulty paying attention over time: Often has difficulty sustaining attention in tasks or play activities. For example, has difficulty remaining focused during lectures, conversations, or lengthy reading.

Not appearing to be listening: Often does not seem to listen when spoken to directly. For example, mind seems elsewhere, even in the absence of any obvious distraction.

Failing to follow through with teachers' or parents' requests: Often does not follow through on instructions and fails to finish schoolwork, chores, or duties in the workplace. For example, starts tasks but quickly loses focus and is easily sidetracked.

Trouble organizing work, often giving the impression of not having heard the teacher's instructions: Often has difficulty organizing tasks and activities. For example, difficulty managing sequential tasks; difficulty keeping materials and belongings in order; messy, disorganized work; has poor time management; fails to meet deadlines.

Avoiding tasks that require sustained attention: Often avoids, dislikes, or is reluctant to engage in tasks that require sustained mental effort. For example, schoolwork or homework; for older adolescents and adults, preparing reports, completing forms, reviewing lengthy papers.

Losing materials necessary to complete tasks: Often loses things necessary for tasks or activities. For example, school materials, pencils, books, tools, wallets, keys, paperwork, eyeglasses, mobile telephones.

Becoming easily distracted: Is often easily distracted by extraneous stimuli. For example, for older adolescents and adults, may include unrelated thoughts.

Forgetfulness in day-to-day activities: Is often forgetful in daily activities. For example, doing chores, running errands; for older adolescents and adults, returning calls, paying bills, keeping appointments.

Hyperactivity

Excessive restlessness or fidgety behavior: Often fidgets with or taps hands or feet or squirms in seat.

Inability to stay seated: Often leaves seat in situations when remaining seated is expected. For example, leaves his or her place in the classroom, in the office or other workplace, or in other situations that require remaining in place.

Running or climbing that is inappropriate: Often runs about or climbs in situations where it is inappropriate. (Note: in adolescents or adults, may be limited to feeling restless.)

Inability to sustain quiet leisure activities: Often unable to play or engage in leisure activities quietly.

Driven behavior, as if "on the go" all the time: Acting as if "driven by a motor." For example, is uncomfortable or unable to be still for extended time, as in restaurants, meetings; may be experienced by others as being restless or difficult to keep up with.

Excessive talking: Can't seem to stop talking, even after several warnings.

Impulsive behavior: Acts without thinking.

Frequently calling out in class (without raising hand, yelling out an answer before a question is finished): Often blurts out an answer before a question has been completed. For example, completes people's sentences; cannot wait for turn in conversation.

Difficulty waiting for his or her turn in group settings: For example, while waiting in line.

Frequent intrusive behavior or interrupting of others: Often interrupts or intrudes on others. For example, butts into conversations, games, or activities; may start using other people's things without asking or receiving permission; for adolescents and adults, may intrude into or take over what others are doing.

Twelve Questions to Consider

A Checklist for Parents

❑ Does my child fidget a lot?

✓ Kids with ADHD simply can't sit still. They run around, fidget, and squirm in their chair when forced to sit. These extra bursts of energy they seem to exhibit can make it difficult for them to play quietly or engage calmly in leisure activities.

❏ Does my child have a short attention span for routine everyday tasks?

✓ Kids with ADHD have a difficult time with tasks that may seem mundane to them, and they need stimulation or excitement in order to stay engaged. Many can pay attention just fine for things that are new, novel, interesting, highly stimulating, or frightening. But in general, they struggle to pay attention, even when someone is speaking directly to them. They'll say they heard you, but they won't be able to repeat what you just said. In addition, kids with ADHD may avoid tasks that require sustained mental effort, such as paying attention in class or doing homework.

❏ Is my child easily distracted?

✓ Kids with ADHD tend to notice more in their environment than others, which makes them easily distracted by outside stimuli, such as light, sounds, smells, certain tastes, or even the clothes they wear. Their keen sensitivity causes them to get off task easily.

❑ Is my child disorganized?

✓ Most people with ADHD tend to struggle with organization of time and space. They tend to be late and have trouble completing tasks on time. Many things get done at the last moment or even later. They also tend to struggle to keep their spaces tidy, especially their rooms, book bags, filing cabinets, drawers, closets, and paperwork.

❑ Is my child forgetful?

✓ Kids with ADHD may be forgetful in daily activities. They may forget to do chores or their homework. They may also lose things often, such as toys.

❑ Does my child procrastinate?

✓ Tasks and duties get put off until the last moment. Things tend not to get done until there are deadlines or someone else is mad at them for not doing it.

❑ Is my child impulsive?

✓ Many people with ADHD have issues with judgment and impulse control and struggle not to say or do things without fully thinking them through. They also have a harder time learning from their mistakes.

❑ Do I notice excessive "self-focused" behavior in my child?

✓ A common sign of ADHD is what looks like an inability to recognize other people's needs and desires. Are they interrupting others or having trouble waiting their turn? Self-focused behavior may also cause them to butt into conversations or games they're not part of, and they may have trouble waiting their turn during classroom activities.

❑ Does my child appear to be in constant emotional turmoil?

✓ Kids with ADHD may have trouble keeping their emotions in check. They may have outbursts of anger at inappropriate times. For example, preschoolers and early elementary–age children may have temper tantrums.

❑ Does my child make careless mistakes and have trouble getting and staying organized?

✓ Children with ADHD may have trouble following instructions that require planning or executing a plan. This can then lead to careless mistakes, but it doesn't indicate laziness or a lack of intelligence. Children with ADHD may have trouble keeping track of tasks and activities. This can cause problems at school because they can find it hard to prioritize homework, school projects, and other assignments.

❑ Does my child daydream a lot?

✓ Loud, rambunctious behavior isn't the only sign of ADHD. Sometimes being quieter and less involved than other kids is a clue. A child with ADHD may stare into space, daydream, and ignore what's going on around him/her.

❑ Does my child show six or more of these symptoms in multiple settings?

✓ A child with ADHD will show symptoms of the condition in more than one setting. For instance, they may show lack of focus both in school and at home.

ADHD Symptoms in Preschoolers

Spotting ADHD in this age group is often tricky since most preschoolers are so full of energy. Running, jumping, and climbing is common behavior. Here's the difference: Their hyper behavior is on "hyperdrive!" In other words, it's extreme. Here's what parents should look for:

- Extreme energy
- Extreme lack of concentration
- Extreme fixation on things that interest them, like certain toys or video games

ADHD Symptoms in Elementary-Age Kids

This disorder will show during the school-age years. Parents may notice other symptoms, too. Basically, kids with ADHD may be unable to focus and may have trouble making good decisions or planning things. They may also have more trouble than other kids their age with:

- Sharing
- Taking turns
- Letting others talk
- Finishing homework or chores

• Keeping track of things like homework and books

ADHD Symptoms in Adolescents

As children with ADHD get older, they often won't have as much self-control as other children their own age, which can make them seem immature compared to their peers. Here are some of the things adolescents with ADHD struggle with:

• Focusing on schoolwork and assignments
• Reading social cues
• Compromising with peers
• Maintaining personal hygiene
• Doing risky things like using alcohol and drugs
• Time management
• Driving safely

CHAPTER 2

ADHD Mythbusters

What ADHD Is and Isn't ... and What Every Parent Must Do

Jamal was muscular and tall for his age, and he looked much older than other thirteen-year-olds at his school. Yet the physical advantage most boys would die to have ended up working against this Minneapolis middle-schooler. Teachers and other adults thought Jamal was much older than he was, so they were often shocked by his immaturity—especially his lack of a social filter and his "childish" inhibitions.

"Go away," he told his math teacher when she stopped by his desk to pick up a test. "I'm not finished."

"Sorry, Jamal," she said tenderly, "but it's a timed exam, and the time is up. You've got to hand it in—otherwise, you'll receive a zero."

"No," he insisted. "I need to finish. Just go away!"

With half the class giggling and the other half gasping in shock, Jamal's teacher folded her arms and locked eyes with the boy. "Not appropriate," she said. "Which means detention for you. I won't ask you again: Hand in your test paper!"

Jamal turned away and looked out the window, seeming to ignore her.

The instructor bent down. "Jamal," she said, "look at me."

Silence.

"Jamal," she said again, "I need you to give me your paper—*now*!"

The boy put his head on his desk and closed his eyes.

"Jamal," the teacher snapped. She reached down and touched Jamal's shoulder.

Suddenly, the boy sat up, jerked away and ran out the classroom door—leaving his classmates stunned.

Later, the phone call to Jamal's mom, Marie, was even more confusing.

"I'm so sorry," Marie said, "but I hope you'll understand what's going on with my son."

Jamal's teacher wasn't cutting any slack: "Thanks, but disrespect is off limits and will never, ever be tolerated in my classroom."

"I understand," Marie said, "but Jamal has ADHD, which means—"

"Which means he needs more discipline," the teacher interrupted. "More guidance from his parents."

"No," Marie said, "I was going to say 'empathy.'"

"Look," the teacher said, "if we're going to talk 'empathy,' please, please understand what teachers like me are up against: a big classroom filled with kids who need guidance...yet who don't always want to listen and respect those who lead them. The thing is, if discipline breaks down, everything falls apart."

Marie took a deep breath. "Again, I understand," she said, "and I really am sorry for Jamal's difficult behavior. He simply can't talk to others that way, and his therapist is working with him—giving him some one-on-one coaching and behavioral therapy. But I need you to hear what's going on: It's a challenge for Jamal to control his actions the way you and I can. His brain is wired differently."

Misunderstanding the ADHD Child

Plenty of well-meaning folks—including teachers and parents—mistakenly believe that individuals with ADHD can control their powers of attention, often thinking, *If they'd exercise a little self-discipline and just try harder...* No doubt you've probably received an earful of advice, including this line: "Toe the line and stand your ground. Eventually, most kids outgrow the condition."

Nothing can be further from the truth.

Ongoing research reveals that symptoms of ADHD are the result of neurological differences rather than misbehavior. Medical professionals have confirmed that children with ADHD have a physiological inability to control their focus the way those without the disorder can. According to Edward M. Halloway, a psychiatrist and leading ADHD expert, "telling someone with ADHD to try harder is no more helpful than telling someone who is nearsighted to squint harder. It [misses] the biological point."[1]

Yet there's good news for the more than 6.1 million American children diagnosed with ADHD and the families who are helping them navigate the disorder.[2] Recent advances in brain imaging demystify the illness and finally make clear what medical experts have known all along: ADHD is real, and it can be successfully treated. For example, neuroimaging illustrates that long-term incentives simply have less impact on the brain's reward circuitry in those with ADHD.[3] In other words, a child with ADHD may gravitate to an immediate attraction, such as playing a video game, and neglect studying for a math test, which would later result in a better grade. Or in the case of Jamal (in the opening story), judgment and impulse control is a challenge for him. The middle-schooler struggles to not say or do things without fully thinking them through. He also has a harder time learning from his mistakes.

Neuropsychiatrist Daniel G. Amen, M.D., believes that brain imaging offers a big step in understanding and healing ADHD in kids like Jamal. Dr. Amen explains that ADHD affects five key regions of the brain:

- The prefrontal cortex and cerebellum: the area of the brain that controls concentration, attention span, judgment, organization, planning, and impulse control
- The anterior cingulate gyrus: the area of the brain that acts as a "gear shifter" and a "place of error detector"
- The temporal lobes: the area of the brain that controls memory, learning, and emotional reactions
- The basal ganglia: the area of the brain that produces the neurotransmitter dopamine that drives the prefrontal cortex
- The deep limbic system: the area of the brain that is involved with setting emotional tone and bonding[4]

"We can see it in the brain," Amen writes in his book *Healing ADHD.*[5] "Brain imaging research conducted at my clinic and at other centers around the world have uncovered the ADHD brain."[6] Based on research with tens of thousands of ADHD patients and using brain imaging called SPECT (single photon emission computed tomography), Amen has been able to see areas of vulnerability in the ADHD brain and why it has such a negative impact on learning, behavior, and emotions. "Humans have an innate distrust of the intangible," Amen explains, "but seeing the ADHD brain can cause the destructive myths and prejudices to fade away."[7]

Yet despite all that physicians have learned about ADHD—and how to treat it successfully—misinformation has prevented sufferers and their families from finding practical solutions that can improve their lives. Children with ADHD, particularly when they are left undiagnosed and untreated, are subjected to a nearly constant flow of negative messaging, especially in the classroom. Here's how Gail Saltz, M.D., a psychiatrist and clinical associate professor of psychiatry at the Weill Cornell Medical Center, assesses the problem:

> The child with ADHD can be a disruption—speaking out at the wrong time, fidgeting, disrupting the

flow of class and generally contributing to a chaotic environment for other students. It's easy to sympathize with the frustration of teachers trying to keep a herd of children on task. The unfortunate impact on the child who is the recipient of so much negative feedback, however, can be injury to self-esteem and squelching of any kind of love for learning. These lively children feel they're constantly being told, "No—what you are doing, thinking, and feeling is wrong: don't do that, sit down, calm down, be quiet."

There is a movement among clinicians to rename ADHD "executive function disorder," and when we consider ADHD from the standpoint of biology—rather than from the subjective observation of seemingly unruly schoolchildren—that name change makes a great deal of sense. What is actually happening in the brains of people with ADHD or executive function disorder is a veering from the norm in the communication between the portions of the brain that execute goals and tasks and those that ponder ideas and look inward in less specifically goal-oriented ways.[8]

How Their World Looks and Feels

Saltz points out that reading can be particularly agonizing for the child with ADHD. "When faced with a pile of academic reading for school," she explains, "many children with ADHD will read a sentence, a paragraph, or a page and realize that although their eyes were scanning the words, their brains were utterly disengaged. Adding to these children's difficulties, some researchers believe that as many as 40 percent of children with ADHD also have dyslexia."[9]

From time to time, every kid gets bored with reading assignments and ends up wrestling with a wandering mind or words that seem to swim all over the page. Yet students with ADHD often experience "distraction on steroids." Comprehending what they're reading can be a big challenge because they have difficulty (1) sustaining their attention span, (2) staying focused on a given task, and (3) managing their tendency to daydream.

Medical professionals have determined that the problem is not one of language processing; rather, it is purely one of wavering focus. Students may demonstrate laser-beam focus on subjects that genuinely interest them. Yet tasks (or reading material) they find irrelevant or boring often drift away with their wandering minds.

Related to the issue of focus is the considerable challenge of getting and staying organized. Dr. Amen explains that most people with ADHD have difficulty with executive function, which is housed in the prefrontal cortex of the brain and is responsible for planning. Assessing the time and steps needed to complete a task, as well as multitasking, can be negatively impacted by poor executive functioning. This is why they are too often labeled with so many unflattering words: slow, lazy, spacey, unmotivated, scatterbrained, forgetful, airy. Some kids feel as if they are always running behind on something. These hurdles—attentional and organizational—are central to the experience of having ADHD. They can be treated, but they will always be a part of the person's neurological makeup.

The challenges that people with ADHD face are not only academic; their greatest struggles are often emotional in nature. Here's what Amen's SPECT findings have uncovered: At rest and during concentration there is increased activity in the basal ganglia, an area associated with anxiety.[10] Primary symptoms include inattentiveness, distractibility, disorganization, anxiety, tension, a tendency to predict the worst, freeze in test-taking situations, and a tendency toward social anxiety.

LET'S GO DEEPER

UNDERSTANDING AND LOVING THE ADHD CHILD

In the remainder of this chapter, we will...

▶ Separate ADHD myths from the truth

▶ Explore alternative treatment options: education, support, exercise, and nutrition

▶ Examine medications that effectively treat ADHD

According to Saltz, it's unclear whether the strong incidence of anxiety in children is due to a difference in the brain that causes both problems, or whether some perception of falling behind is present because ADHD leads to anxiety. "Anxiety alone can lead to inattentiveness, because a child is preoccupied with worrisome thoughts," she says. "But if the child has ADHD, then even once the anxiety is treated they will still be inattentive. Children with both anxiety and ADHD tend to be more inattentive but less impulsive than those with ADHD alone."[11]

Dr. Saltz also points out that there is a strong association between ADHD, risk-taking, and lack of impulse control. "This makes great sense when we think of ADHD in terms of the [brain's] deficit in executive function."[12]

Debunking the ADHD Myths

Myth: All kids with ADHD are hyperactive.

Fact: Some children with ADHD are hyperactive, but many others with attention problems are not. Children with ADHD who are inattentive but not overly active may appear to be spacey and unmotivated.

Myth: Kids with ADHD can never pay attention.

Fact: Children with ADHD are often able to concentrate on activities they enjoy. But no matter how hard they try, they have trouble maintaining focus when the task at hand is boring or repetitive.

Myth: Kids with ADHD could behave better if they wanted to.

Fact: Children with ADHD may do their best to be good but still find themselves unable to sit still, stay quiet, or pay attention. They may appear disobedient, but that doesn't mean they're acting out on purpose.

Myth: Kids will eventually grow out of ADHD.

Fact: ADHD often continues into adulthood, so don't wait for your child to outgrow the problem. Treatment can help your child learn to manage and minimize the symptoms.

Myth: Medication is the best treatment option for ADHD.

Fact: Medication is often prescribed, but it might not be the best option for your child. Effective treatments for ADHD include education, behavior therapy, support at home and school, exercise, and proper nutrition.

Managing ADHD

Is medicine the answer? How about alternative remedies— such as the kind that focus on nutrition and exercise? Or maybe a combination of the two?

Treating ADHD doesn't necessarily mean prescribing children medication. In fact, too many kids, especially boys who are merely rambunctious, are being given the drugs with just cursory evaluations, insists William Pollack, an assistant clinical professor at Harvard Medical School.[13]

In his ongoing research into boyhood, Pollack has found anecdotal evidence that Ritalin renders some kids less interested in pursuing creative opportunities. One boy he studied had been active in his school's science club. After he was put on Ritalin, he felt like the spark inside him was extinguished.

He lost interest in the science club and dropped out. Eventually, he stopped taking Ritalin, returned to the club, and developed a flashlight alarm system that won a major science competition.[14]

Another subject in Dr. Pollack's research is a math whiz in his forties who was hyperactive as a child. As an adult, the man earned several hundred million dollars developing computer technology. "His ideas come to him in a flash," explains Pollack. "He feels that if he had been given Ritalin as a child, he'd have just ended up as a teaching assistant in some science course."[15]

There's no doubt that, for many children, the right ADHD medication makes a huge difference in improving their behavior; we can't overestimate its importance. According to Amen, "People who have mild to even moderate ADHD may be able to treat the disorder through natural means."[16] He believes that people with more severe forms of ADHD often need medication. "It is usually not the first thing to do," he says, "but when necessary and if prescribed properly, it can make a huge positive difference."[17]

We believe it's essential that we evaluate five key aspects of a child's life before turning to prescription drugs:

Diet: Is your child getting the nutrition he needs?

Aerobic health: Is your child getting regular aerobic exercise?

Need for comfort and relaxation: Is your child getting ample time to relax and have fun?

Need for sleep: Is your child getting the sleep she needs every day?

Overall lifestyle: Is your child living a balanced life?

While ADHD meds aren't the cure-all, they can be a must for some children. Our advice? Talk with your family physician and a licensed therapist. Get a complete physical and full evaluation before pursuing medication.

Serving Up a Healthy ADHD Diet

Ideally, our eating habits should help the brain work better and help us to have better focus. In fact, most health experts concur that what children eat and drink can have both a positive and a negative effect on their minds—especially for kids with symptoms of ADHD.[18] So, here's what parents need to focus on:

- ✓ Overall nutrition: The assumption is that some foods we give our kids can make their symptoms better or worse. They also might not be eating some things that could help make symptoms better.
- ✓ Supplementation diet: With this plan, you add vitamins, minerals, or other nutrients. The idea is

that it could help your child make up for not getting enough of these through what they eat. Sup-
porters of these diets think that if children don't
get enough of certain nutrients, their symptoms
may be augmented.

✓ Elimination diets: These involve not eating foods
   or ingredients that might be triggering certain
   behaviors in your child or making their symptoms
   worse.

Eat Nutritious Food

A high-protein diet. Beans, cheese, eggs, meat, and nuts
can be good sources of protein. Eat these kinds of foods in the
morning and for after-school snacks. It may improve your
child's concentration and possibly make ADHD medications work longer.

More complex carbohydrates: These are the good kids.
Load up on vegetables and some fruits, including oranges,
tangerines, pears, grapefruit, apples, and kiwi. Have them
eat this type of food in the evening, and it may help them
sleep.

More omega-3 fatty acids: You can find these in tuna,
salmon, and other cold-water white fish. Walnuts, Brazil nuts,
and olive and canola oils are other foods with these in them.

You could also give your child an omega-3 fatty acid supplement. The FDA approved an omega compound called Vayarin as part of an ADHD management strategy.

Eating smart will improve your child's wellbeing. Not only is a well-balanced diet the foundation to good health for every man, woman, and child, it's especially crucial for the kid with ADHD. Certain foods and drinks can stimulate our bodies and actually trigger anxiety. Think about the caffeine, sugar, and fat you may be putting into your kid's body. Think about how you feel after you put these things in your own. You end up crashing and feeling stressed...right?

Here are some important dietary steps that we guarantee will reap profound benefits:

Watch Out for Caffeine

Your child is probably getting more of this than you think, especially in soft drinks like Coke or Mountain Dew.

What happens inside our body: Caffeine stimulates the nervous system, which—as you know—triggers the release of adrenaline, making you feel nervous and jittery. Some medical professionals claim that there is a link between caffeine intake and high blood pressure, as well as high cholesterol levels.[19]

Our advice: eliminate caffeinated drinks.

Reduce Their Sugar Intake

Your child's craving for sweets starts at an early age. Yet understand this: Sugar has no essential nutrients. It gives us a quick boost of energy, and then we crash.

What happens inside our body? Our adrenal glands become exhausted—i.e., the crash—and we begin feeling irritable and usually have difficulty concentrating. We may even feel a bit depressed. In addition, consuming large quantities of sugar is bad for the pancreas, and it increases the possibility of developing diabetes.

Our advice: keep your child's blood sugar constant, and never use sugar as a "pick me up."

Cut Back on Fatty Foods

Avoid giving your child foods rich in saturated fats. Fats cause obesity and put unnecessary stress on the cardiovascular system. High fat is believed to cause breast, colon, and prostate cancers.

Your ADHD Child Should Eat This, Not That ...
Foods to Eat
Whole grains promote the production of the brain neurotransmitter serotonin, which increases your sense of well-being.

Green, yellow, and orange vegetables are all rich in minerals, vitamins, and phytochemicals, which boost immune response and protect against disease. Eating more vegetables can increase our brain's serotonin production. This increase is due to improved absorption of the amino acid L-tryptophan. (Vegetables contain the natural, safe form of L-tryptophan.) Meats contain natural L-tryptophan also, but when you eat meat, the L-tryptophan has to compete with so many other amino acids for absorption that it loses out. Your body can better absorb L-tryptophan when you eat vegetables.

Eat more fiber. Stress results in cramps and constipation. Eat more fiber to keep your digestive system moving. Your meals should provide at least 25 grams of fiber per day. Fruits, vegetables and grains are excellent sources. For breakfast, eat whole fruits instead of just juice; have whole-grain cereals and fiber-fortified muffins.

Eat a meal high in carbohydrates. Carbohydrates trigger release of the brain neurotransmitter serotonin, which soothes you. Good sources of carbohydrates include rice, pasta, potatoes, breads, air-popped popcorn, and low-cal cookies. Experts suggest that the carbohydrates present in a baked potato or a cup of spaghetti or white rice are enough to relieve the anxiety of a stressful day.

Foods to Avoid
Fried foods and foods rich in fat are very immune-depressing, especially when stress is suppressing the immune system as well.
Reduce animal foods. High-protein foods elevate brain levels of dopamine and norepinephrine, both of which are associated with higher levels of anxiety and stress.
Avoid foods that are high in sugar.

When Pharmaceutical Drugs Are the Best First Option

As we treat ADHD in children, we should implement a complete wellness program that includes proper diet, exercise, and supplements—all beginning with a physical and mental evaluation.

Medication is an important issue to consider. While kids with mild to moderate ADHD may benefit from natural alternatives (such as the options highlighted above), children with severe ADHD often need medication.

Here's a sample of the types of drugs that are commonly prescribed for ADHD:

MEDICATIONS	INDICATIONS	ADVERSE REACTIONS
Trade Names: Adderall, Adderall XR Therapeutic Class: Stimulants Pharmacologic Class: Amphetamines Dosages (tablets): 5 mg–40 mg	Attention deficit hyperactivity disorder (ADHD) Narcolepsy	Central Nervous System: headache, insomnia, drowsiness, mood swings Gastrointestinal: nausea, abdominal pain, decreased appetite, weight loss
MEDICATIONS	INDICATIONS	ADVERSE REACTIONS
Trade Names: Concerta, Metadate CD, Metadate ER, Quillivant XR, Ritalin, Ritalin LA, Ritalin-SR Therapeutic Class: CNS stimulants Pharmacologic Class: Piperidine derivatives Available Forms: Oral solution (Methylin): 5 mg/5 mL, 10 mg/5 mL Tablets (chewable): 2.5 mg, 5 mg, 10 mg Tablets (Ritalin): 5 mg, 10 mg, 20 mg	Attention deficit hyperactivity disorder (ADHD) Narcolepsy	Central Nervous System: nervousness, headache, insomnia, seizures, tics, dizziness, akathisia, dyskinesia, drowsiness, mood swings Cardiovascular: palpitations, tachycardia, arrhythmias, hypertension Gastrointestinal: nausea, abdominal pain, anorexia, decreased appetite, vomiting Respiratory: cough, upper respiratory tract infection

MEDICATIONS	INDICATIONS	ADVERSE REACTIONS
Trade Name: Strattera Therapeutic Class: ADHD drugs Pharmacologic Class: Selective norepinephrine reuptake inhibitors Dosages (capsules): 10 mg, 18 mg, 25 mg, 40 mg, 60 mg, 80 mg, 100 mg	ADHD Nocturnal enuresis	Central Nervous System: headache, insomnia, somnolence, crying, irritability, mood swings, pyrexia, fatigue, sedation, depression, tremors, early-morning awakening, paresthesia, abnormal dreams, sleep disorder Cardiovascular: orthostatic hypotension, tachycardia, hypertension, palpitations, hot flashes Genitourinary: abdominal pain, constipation, dyspepsia nausea, vomiting, decreased appetite, dry mouth

Any mental disorder also has a strong underlying bio-chemical disturbance and responds well to medication. Except in relatively minor cases, the effective use of medication is essential for effective treatment in the early stages of panic and other anxiety disorders. Proper medication, combined with cognitive-behavioral psychotherapy, will ensure a complete cure in most cases.

CHAPTER 3

Four Steps to Getting an Accurate Diagnosis

Pinpointing Your Child's Unique Needs Is Crucial to Finding Relief

The ADHD evaluation felt excruciating to Rae, but she knew she had to commit every ounce of energy to getting help for her daughter—which meant swallowing her pride and pushing back her fear of letting doctors label her kid with a disorder. *We need some answers,* Rae thought as she sat in the waiting room of the clinical psychiatrist to whom the family doctor had referred her. *I need to know what's holding Melody back at school. What's going on in that otherwise beautiful mind of hers?*

On more days than Rae could count, Melody seemed aloof, preferring to be alone, and at times she was a bit depressed. Lately, the nine-year-old was coming up short in all her lessons—including her favorite: music. That's what concerned Rae the most. Melody was a promising pianist and seemed to gravitate to all things musical.

No doubt she's stressed, Rae thought to herself. After twelve years of marriage, Rae's husband had recently packed his bags and left, which was a crushing blow to Melody.

Yet Rae couldn't help but wonder if anything else was going on with her daughter. Is she battling a learning disability or a medical condition? Or could it be what I've suspected all along and what I've got to accept: that my daughter has ADHD?

The final push to get answers had begun with a note from Melody's teacher:

> Academically, your daughter just isn't progressing with the rest of the class. She's falling farther and farther behind, and she seems overwhelmed. Socially, I'm observing that she's not at the same maturity level as other girls her age. She's often picked on by other kids and labeled "weird" and "babyish." Of course, I do my best to put a stop to any kind of name-calling. I'm just so concerned about Melody and think you need to have some psychological evaluation conducted on her. There's a chance she's on the spectrum.

"Miss Rae," a voice blurted, jolting the mom back into the moment. She looked up and saw the clinical psychiatrist smiling, standing next to Melody—who looked awkward and uncomfortable, like she'd just endured seven hours under a dentist's drill.

Yep, I know that look, Rae thought to herself. This whole process feels like a root canal.

"Let's switch," the doctor said warmly. "I'd like Melody to have a seat here in the waiting room, and Rae, come on into my office."

Once inside, the doctor got right down to business, never mincing words or pulling any punches. "Your homelife is definitely a stressful place these days, and I think both Melody and you could benefit from therapy—but let's focus on your daughter," the doctor said. "After running the tests, I have some answers for you: I have diagnosed Melody with Type 2—Inattentive ADHD."

The words hung in the air for a moment, and Rae suddenly felt a mix of emotions rushing from her head all the way to her toes: relief, determination, hope...fear, uncertainty, shame.

On the one hand, Rae and Melody finally had some conclusive, long-awaited answers they'd been seeking. Yet at the same time, the diagnosis was official. A clinical assessment had been handed down—a mental disorder was determined. For the rest of Melody's life, this precious young lady would live with the label ADHD.

"I can tell you're not entirely comfortable with this," the doctor said to Rae. "But I assure you, everything is going to be okay. Your daughter finally has some answers to the struggles she has endured for so long. We will customize a plan and treat her. Melody's life is going to improve."

Rae leaned back in her chair and looked out the window. Yes—we finally have some answers. Will our lives improve? I hope so.

If You Suspect ADHD Is the Issue

As Rae and Melody discovered, the search for answers begins with a routine visit to a primary-care physician and then involves a few more steps after that. They endured appointments with ADHD specialists, time spent talking, taking tests, and getting a detailed analysis of the unique inner workings of Melody's mind.

Quite possibly, this is the same path you will follow if you suspect ADHD is the issue.

More than one medical professional will assess your child for ADHD symptoms. The diagnosis will begin with a clinical interview to gather his or her medical history, and then it will be supplemented with neuropsychological testing, which offers greater insight into your child's strengths and weaknesses. Physicians, clinical and school psychologists, clinical social workers, speech-language pathologists, learning specialists, and educators also may each play an important role in the ADHD evaluation.[1] It is

LET'S GO DEEPER

UNDERSTANDING AND LOVING THE ADHD CHILD

In the remainder of this chapter, we will...

▶ Move through the steps of getting an ADHD evaluation

▶ Discuss what medical professionals sometimes overlook

▶ Explore the different types of ADHD

essential to identify co-existing (or comorbid) conditions with overlapping symptoms, such as learning disabilities, mood disorders, or autism spectrum disorder.[2]

But as you begin this process, here's what you must steer clear of: relying solely on medical professionals who are not trained in the nuances of ADHD and who are not equipped to perform the in-depth evaluation that's needed. Family doctors, who aren't always adequately trained in this area, sometimes diagnose children with ADHD when there really may be another condition going on or, in fact, nothing at all. Like most mental health disorders, ADHD is not black and white. It is a perplexing condition that can affect the academic and social lives of affected children, possibly into adulthood.[3]

Yet all too often, parents are at the mercy of overworked family doctors who simply don't have the time to sort through details of a very complex condition. In some cases, they run the risk of a misdiagnosis...right along with a prescription for meds that may not effectively treat their child's unique condition.

Tip: As you launch your search, avoid a cursory evaluation by a pediatrician or primary care physician who is quick to prescribe a prescription for stimulants.

Just because a kid can't sit still or his or her grades are slipping doesn't mean ADHD is the culprit. The symptoms must be present every day for a long period of time and must lead to an impairment of a child's life for it to be true ADHD. That's how it was for Melody and for so many children just like her. In fact, ADHD is a common condition that affects 4.4 percent of adults and 9.4 percent of children, but it's highly complex and requires a much deeper investigation than just a brief office visit and a one-size-fits-all treatment plan.[4]

A recent study conducted by the U.S. Centers for Disease Control and Prevention (CDC) showed that 11 percent of school-age children in the United States have received a diagnosis of ADHD.[5]

What has alarmed many is the way the rate has climbed. According to the study, the rate has skyrocketed 16 percent over the past decade. The rise was most dramatic among high school–aged boys, with an estimated one in five diagnosed with ADHD.

Here's how you can avoid what health care professionals often overlook and ensure your child receives an accurate diagnosis.

Steps to Getting an Accurate Diagnosis

STEP 1: The Initial Consultation with Your Pediatrician

A primary-care doctor serves as a diagnostical entry point for children. Your doctor will ask you detailed questions about your child's general health, educational performance (specifically, scholastic underachievement), and overall psychological wellbeing, and will then proceed with a complete physical exam, including bloodwork, vision, and hearing screenings. Also, the FDA has approved the use of the

Neuropsychiatric EEG-Based Assessment Aid (NEBA) System, a noninvasive scan that measures theta and beta brain waves. Some pediatricians incorporate this test in their evaluations. The theta/beta ratio has been shown to be higher in children and adolescents with ADHD than in children without it.[6] The scan, approved for use in those aged six to seventeen, is meant to be used as a part of a complete medical and psychological exam.

In addition, your pediatrician will work up a complete medical history to screen for other conditions that may affect your child's behavior. Those that could mimic ADHD or cause ADHD-like behaviors include recent major life changes (such as divorce, a death in the family, or a recent move), undetected seizures, thyroid issues, problems sleeping, anxiety, and depression.[7]

While launching your search for answers can feel overwhelming, rest assured you're doing the right thing, and health care providers are there to help. According to the American Academy of Pediatrics, "Clinicians are charged to work with families and children, in collaboration with school personnel, to determine whether or not a child has ADHD and any possible coexisting conditions, to identify target treatment outcomes, and to assure that the child with ADHD functionally improves over time."[8]

As thorough as these initial examinations may be, they serve only as the entry points for evaluating your child for ADHD. Unlike other medical conditions, ADHD is not caused by a simple, single event, nor can a blood test provide definitive proof. Instead, diagnosing it is based on observations from you, teachers, health care providers, and other caregivers.

STEP 2: Meeting with a Specialist

Next, your child will be referred to a specialist—usually a psychologist or psychiatrist, possibly both. (There's always the possibly that you'll end up consulting with more than one professional.) During this critical phase of the process,

QUICK FACTS ABOUT ADHD

▶ ADHD is the most commonly studied and diagnosed psychiatric disorder in children. It is considered a neurobehavioral developmental disorder.

▶ ADHD affects approximately 3 to 7 percent of all children globally, with symptoms typically presenting before the age of seven.

▶ Boys are two to four times more likely than girls to be diagnosed with ADHD.

▶ Scientists are not sure exactly what causes ADHD, although many studies suggest that genetics and brain chemistry play a large role. It is thought that ADHD may result from a combination of factors, including genetics, brain injuries, nutrition, environmental factors, and/or social influences.[9]

mental health professionals will guide you through question-naires regarding your son's or daughter's behavior in the class-room and at home. Information they gather will help them determine if your child is indeed suffering from ADHD.

Health care providers use the guidelines in the American Psychiatric Association's *Diagnostic and Statistical Manual of Mental Disorders*, Fifth Edition (DSM-5) to help diagnose ADHD.[10] This diagnostic standard helps ensure that your child is appropriately evaluated and treated.

As we discussed in Chapter 1, kids with ADHD show a persistent pattern of inattention and/or hyperactivity that interferes with functioning or development. In fact, the symptoms associated with ADHD can interfere with attaining many of the normal developmental milestones of childhood and adolescence that primary care clinicians monitor, such as academic, fine motor, and social and adaptive skills. As a result, children with ADHD often experience school failure, poor family and peer relations, low self-esteem, and other emotional, behavioral, and learning problems.[11]

Here's a quick summary of what we unpacked in the previous chapter, as well as what mental health professionals are looking for:[12]

Inattention: Six or more symptoms of inattention for children up to age sixteen, or five or more for people age seventeen and older; symptoms of inattention have been present for at least six months, and are inappropriate for developmental level:

- Often fails to give close attention to details or makes careless mistakes in schoolwork, at work, or with other activities
- Often has trouble holding attention on tasks or play activities
- Often does not seem to listen when spoken to directly
- Often does not follow through on instructions and fails to finish schoolwork, chores, or duties in the workplace (e.g., loses focus, easily sidetracked)
- Often has trouble organizing tasks and activities.
- Often avoids, dislikes, or is reluctant to do tasks that require mental effort over a long period of time (such as schoolwork or homework)
- Often loses things necessary for tasks and activities (e.g., school materials, pencils, books, tools, wallets, keys, paperwork, eyeglasses, mobile telephones)

• Is often easily distracted
• Is often forgetful in daily activities

Hyperactivity and Impulsivity: Six or more symptoms of hyperactivity-impulsivity for children up to age sixteen years, or five or more for people age seventeen and older; symptoms of hyperactivity-impulsivity have been present for at least six months to an extent that is disruptive and inappropriate for the person's developmental level:

• Often fidgets, taps hands or feet, or squirms in seat
• Often leaves seat in situations when remaining seated is expected
• Often runs about or climbs in situations where it is not appropriate (adolescents or adults may be limited to feeling restless)
• Often unable to play or take part in leisure activities quietly
• Is often "on the go," acting as if "driven by a motor"
• Often talks excessively
• Often blurts out an answer before a question has been completed

- Often has trouble waiting their turn
- Often interrupts or intrudes on others (e.g., butts into conversations or games)

Before your first visit, many specialists will reach out to people in your child's life who know him or her best—a sibling, a teacher, a coach, or a nanny—and they'll use the interview to determine which, if any, tests might rule out other conditions that may be causing symptoms. They'll ask them

COMMON BEHAVIORS OBSERVED IN CHILDREN WITH ADHD

▶ They are constantly in motion

▶ They squirm and fidget

▶ They make careless mistakes

▶ They often lose things

▶ They often seem to tune out others and not listen

▶ They are easily distracted

▶ They often do not finish tasks

to write a few sentences that capture your child's personality and behaviors, insight that often can't be culled from questionnaires.

During your initial consultation, which may last an hour or longer, your doctor will ask you and your child lots of questions—and they'll often move through psychological checklists as well as feedback and written information from the interviews they conducted. Sometimes, the doctor's office will forward these forms to you before your visit and review them with you at the initial meeting.[13] Other doctors will meet with you first, do the interview, and give you the forms to be filled out before your next appointment.[14]

For example, here's what a teacher wrote about Melody (the nine-year-old in our opening story): "One minute, she is soft-spoken and kind, but then she can shift into a fear-worry spiral in which she becomes oppositional and argumentative. And so often Melody seems to be in her own world in which she doesn't listen to instruction. In fact, she isn't keeping up with the rest of the class, and she refuses to begin assignments that don't interest her. But turn her loose on something that she enjoys, and she's at the head of the class."

This kind of feedback is what professionals call the moral diagnosis, and these one-paragraph narratives give a wide range of input, often revealing a lot about a child who may have ADHD.[15] As specialists work their way through the checklists and clinical interviews, here are the topics they will cover:

Medical History: They'll evaluate a wide range of health-related issues—everything from sleep apnea and thyroid conditions to hormone fluctuations and substance abuse.

Family History: They'll evaluate a family's gene pool, going beyond the immediate family and uncovering possible mental disorders in grandparents, uncles, aunts, and cousins.

Social Behavior: They'll evaluate relationships and inter-personal communication in your child's life—asking you, your child, and those being interviewed to "describe a typical day," to "tell what causes conflict with others," and to share "what makes life peaceful."

A Child's Strengths and Weaknesses: They'll evaluate a child's interests and dislikes, pursuits they excel at, and activities they find challenging.

Academic Progress: They'll evaluate a child's educational experiences, including grades, coursework, and academic records.

By the time the clinical interview is over, most doctors with experience treating people with ADHD will have a good idea of whether your child has the condition. Even so, most will want to back up their opinion with objective proof from tests.

STEP 3: Navigating a Battery of ADHD Tests

It's important to assess three areas of a child's life:

- Biology—the physical processes at work, including genetics, family history, nutritional status, exercise, general health, and sleep
- Psychology—the developmental history, including how a child thinks, the quality of his thoughts, social circle, and possible stress in life
- Spirituality—faith and beliefs, including what gives a child hope as well as her sense of meaning and purpose in life

As kids are evaluated for ADHD, most clinical interviews include completing one or more of the ADHD rating scales, as well as other ADHD tests. A proper ADHD test should do two things: determine whether a person has ADHD, and rule out or identify other problems—learning disabilities, autism, auditory processing disorders, or mood disorders. The clinician will ask about symptoms related to ADHD. In children, many of these characteristics are seen in a school setting, so the clinician will also ask about behavior in school. To help collect this information, the evaluator will often interview parents, teachers, and other caregivers or ask them to fill out special behavioral checklists.[16]

Depending on your doctor's concerns, tests may take from one hour to more than eight hours to complete and may require several appointments.

Here's a list of tests medical professionals may use to diagnose your child:

ADHD Rating Scales: These questionnaires can identify specific symptoms of ADHD that may not emerge in the clinical interview. Answers to the questions can reveal how well a child functions at school and home. The scales are specifically formatted for children, adolescents, and adults.[17]

Intelligence Tests: These are a standard part of most thorough evaluations because they not only measure IQ but can also detect certain learning disabilities common in people with ADHD.

Broad-Spectrum Scales: These screen for social, emotional, and psychiatric problems, and they may be ordered if the doctor suspects that a patient has a mood disorder, obsessive-compulsive disorder, or another condition in addition to ADHD.

Tests of Specific Abilities: These tests evaluate language development, vocabulary, memory, and motor skills. In addition, they are often recommended to screen for learning disabilities or other processing problems. The doctor may decide which tests to do based in part on which kinds of tasks your child finds easy or difficult.

Computer Tests: These are becoming popular because patients enjoy taking them and because they can screen for attention and impulsivity problems, which are common in people with ADHD. These "continuous performance tests" (CPT) challenge the patient to sustain attention. A series of visual targets appear on the screen, and the user responds to prompts while the computer measures his or her ability to stay on task. In practice, some experts have found that these tests are better at identifying impulsive symptoms and less successful at flagging symptoms of inattention.[18]

Brain Wave Test: This was approved by the Federal Drug Administration to assist in the diagnosis of ADHD.[19] In MRI scans comparing the brains of children with ADHD to those without, researchers at Columbia University noted less coordinated brain activity between the two regions involving decision making (the prefrontal cortex) and controlling impulses (the caudate) in children with ADHD.[20]

Brain SPECT Imaging: This is a sophisticated tool and quantitative EEG that can help doctors understand the underlying biology of a patient.[21]

STEP 4: Developing an ADHD Management Action Plan

After the clinical interview and the recommended tests are completed, most doctors will call you into the office to go over the results of your ADHD evaluation. This is the best time to ask the doctor questions. When you leave that appointment, the doctor should have formulated an action plan to manage symptoms, which should include these items:[22]

- ✓ A list of accommodations for school that will help your child perform well
- ✓ A plan for follow-up therapy with a psychologist, therapist, ADHD coach, or another expert
- ✓ Recommendations for ADHD medication, if considered appropriate
- ✓ A schedule of follow-up appointments with the diagnosing physician or your primary care doctor to see how well the treatment plan is working

Rae's daughter Melody endured more than six hours of testing over a one-week period—time well spent, Rae insists. "Our psychiatrist determined that Melody was dealing with Type 3 Overfocused ADHD, which means she is inattentive, has trouble shifting attention, frequently gets stuck in loops of negative thoughts, and is prone to excessive worrying and argumentative behavior. This often triggers physical reactions such as an upset stomach and headaches."

The ADHD action management plan Rae was given included something this weary mom now describes as a "godsend"—a list of accommodations that are helping Melody improve at school. "This single tool has enabled Melody's teachers to understand what's going on with my daughter so they can make accommodations that will help her succeed," Rae says. "So, at the onset of a migraine-like headache or an anxious tummy, Melody is allowed to visit the nurse's office where she can rest in a dark room or spend time with some one-on-one help in the library or in the study hall."

While at first many parents are fearful that a label like "ADHD" may cause more harm than help for a child—that was Rae's initial concern—most discover that an accurate diagnosis can lead to relief on the home front. Life really can get better. "We're learning how to manage ADHD," Rae says. "My daughter is happier, and her life is improving."

Here are other treatment approaches that may be used alone or in combination:[23]

Behavioral Therapy: This refers to techniques that try to improve behavior, usually by rewarding and encouraging desirable behaviors and by discouraging unwanted behaviors and pointing out the consequences.

Cognitive Therapy: This is psychotherapy designed to change thinking to build self-esteem, stop having negative thoughts, and improve problem-solving skills.

Social Skill Training: Developing social skills improves friendships.

Parent Education and Support: Training classes, support groups, and counselors can help to support and teach parents about ADHD, including strategies for dealing with ADHD-related behaviors.

What Health Care Professionals Might Overlook

Here are some critical issues about ADHD that many health care professionals and parents might be missing that could be preventing your child from getting relief.

Overlooking Other Mental Disorders That Could Be at Work

The CDC reports that six of ten children with ADHD have at least one other mental, emotional, or behavioral disorder. According to neuropsychiatrist and ADHD expert Daniel G. Amen, when doctors evaluate a child for ADHD, they must also look for other mental disorders that could be at play: depression, bipolar disorder, anxiety, obsessive-compulsive disorder, and tic disorders (such as Tourette's syndrome).[24] In addition, Dr. Amen recommends a thorough investigation of these possible issues: adjustment disorders or family problems; a history of physical, emotional, or sexual abuse; medical factors; and learning/developmental problems.

Only by understanding everything that may be contributing to symptoms and addressing each of these issues can your child truly get well. Yet too often, doctors diagnose the symptoms but not the underlying problem. Physicians must look for coexisting ADHD. In many cases, when the ADHD is treated, the secondary symptoms also improve.

Not Conducting a Thorough Evaluation

As we said earlier, a fifteen-minute visit with a pediatrician is not enough time to diagnose ADHD. Yet rushed visits aren't uncommon, and they raise the likelihood that your child will be misdiagnosed and that your health care provider will miss a secondary disorder.

Thinking That Hyperactivity Defines Every Child with ADHD

Many people with this condition are never hyperactive. The non-hyperactive or "inattentive" ADHD people are often ignored because they don't bring enough negative attention to themselves. Many of these children, teenagers, or adults earn the unjust labels "willful," "lazy," "unmotivated," or "not that smart." Among the patients at Amen Clinics, inattentive ADHD without hyperactivity tends to be more common in females.

Forgetting That ADHD Is a Brain Issue

Based on brain-imaging studies using a technology called SPECT, which measures blood flow and activity in the brain, Amen Clinics has found that ADHD is associated with abnormal brain patterns. And there isn't just one type. There are seven types of ADHD. Knowing your type is essential to getting the right help for yourself or your child. To discover your type, take the Amen Clinics ADHD Type Test online. It takes just a few minutes.

Overlooking the ADHD–Substance Abuse Connection

Smoking and drug and alcohol abuse are very common problems in teenagers and adults with untreated ADHD. A 2011 study by researchers at Harvard University published in the *Journal of the American Academy of Child & Adolescent Psychiatry* reported that people with the condition are one and a half times more likely to develop substance abuse issues compared with people who don't have ADHD.[25]

Assuming That Stimulants Work on Every Child with ADHD

Stimulant medications can be helpful for some people with ADHD but not for everybody. In fact, giving stimulants to people with certain types of ADHD makes them worse. In addition, according to the neuropsychiatrists at Amen Clinics, taking prescription medication should never be the first or only thing you do to treat a mental health condition.

Head Trauma Can Contribute to the Condition

One of the most common causes of ADHD-like symptoms outside of genetics is head trauma, especially to the prefrontal cortex. SPECT is clearly able to show areas of damage invisible to CAT scans or MRI studies. When the prefrontal cortex is injured, people have more ADHD-like symptoms. Many people—even health care professionals—do not fully understand how head injuries, sometimes even "minor" ones where no loss of consciousness occurs, can alter a person's character and ability to learn.

Forgetting That Biology Matters

It's important that doctors assess what your child eats, how well they sleep, and how much exercise they receive. Each area can have a major impact on their symptoms. Most people with ADHD (but not Type 3 Overfocused) do best with a higher-protein, lower-carbohydrate diet. Getting thirty to forty-five minutes daily of exercise, especially aerobic exercise that increases blood flow to the prefrontal cortex, can be very helpful. Sleep disturbances are very common in people with ADHD. Many have trouble getting to sleep at night and getting up in the morning. Sleep deprivation leads to overall decreased brain activity. In order to optimize brain function, aim for at least seven hours each night.

Underestimating the Effectiveness of Nutritional Supplements

Basic supplements that can benefit people with all types of ADHD include a multivitamin/mineral, omega-3 fatty acids, and vitamin D. There is good scientific evidence that rhodiola extract, green tea, ginseng, and ashwagandha increase focus and attention.

Dismissing the Benefits of Neurofeedback

A very exciting biological treatment for ADHD is neurofeedback. This interactive, non-invasive therapy helps strengthen the brain to achieve a more focused state. Amen Clinics patients who have used neurofeedback therapy have reported enhanced focus, decreased impulsivity, and improved moods.

Thinking That Academic Failure Points to ADHD

Many children with ADHD do well at school because they work hard, and teachers and doctors will not suspect they have the condition.

Thinking That a High IQ Dismisses ADHD

Your child may score well on an IQ test, but her grades may be mediocre and teachers may "diagnose" her as being lazy or undisciplined. An evaluation by an outside psychologist may indicate that she has ADHD and/or a learning disorder.

Sticking with a Doctor You Don't Like

If you don't feel a positive connection with your doctor—if he doesn't seem to respond to you as a person or if he reprimands you for asking too many questions—you won't have confidence in his diagnosis and ADHD treatment won't go well.

Understanding the Different Types of ADHD

Once you receive the official diagnosis of ADHD, it is essential that you learn which type it is. According to the DSM-5, children are usually diagnosed with one of three subcategories of ADHD:

Predominantly Inattentive: A child with this diagnosis presents symptoms that are more inattentive in nature. They are easily distracted, forgetful, have trouble organizing and completing tasks, become bored easily, struggle to follow directions, have difficulty focusing on one thing, daydream and/or have trouble completing or turning in homework assignments. Children with this subtype are less likely to act out or have difficulties getting along with other children. In fact, they tend to be very quiet and are often overlooked. Parents and teachers may not notice that the child has ADHD.

Predominantly Hyperactive-Impulsive: Children who are diagnosed with this type of ADHD may display symptoms such as talking nonstop, fidgeting, and squirming in their seats, have difficulty doing quiet tasks, are very impatient, blurt out inappropriate comments, and act without regard for consequences.

Combined Hyperactive-Impulsive and Inattentive: These children have the symptoms of hyperactivity, impulsivity, and inattention. Most children who are diagnosed with ADHD fall into this category.

Yet Dr. Amen and other neuropsychiatrists—who have spent decades delving into the brain and researching ADHD—have concluded that there are seven distinct types. As Dr. Amen points out, a single treatment plan cannot address the nuances of each distinct type of ADHD. What's more, it is also possible for a child to have more than one type of the disorder. Knowing your child's type is essential to getting the right help.

Here are the seven types of ADHD that health care providers and parents alike must consider as they find solutions for the children in their care:[26]

Type 1: Classic ADHD—inattentive, distractible, disorganized, hyperactive, restless, and impulsive.

Type 2: Inattentive ADHD—inattentive, easily distracted, disorganized, and often described as space cadets, daydreamers, and couch potatoes. Not hyperactive!

Type 3: Overfocused ADHD—inattentive, trouble shifting attention, frequently get stuck in loops of negative thoughts or behaviors, obsessive, excessive worry, inflexible, frequent oppositional and argumentative behavior. May or may not be hyperactive.

Type 4: Temporal Lobe ADHD—inattentive, easily distracted, disorganized, irritable, short fuse, dark thoughts, mood instability, and may struggle with learning disabilities. May or may not be hyperactive.

Type 5: Limbic ADHD—inattentive, easily distracted, disorganized, chronic low-grade sadness or negativity, "glass half empty syndrome," low energy, tends to be more isolated socially, and frequent feelings of hopelessness and worthlessness. May or may not be hyperactive.

Type 6: Ring of Fire ADHD—inattentive, easily distracted, irritable, overly sensitive, cyclical moodiness, and oppositional. May or may not be hyperactive.

Type 7: Anxious ADHD—inattentive, easily distracted, disorganized, anxious, tense, nervous, predicts the worst, gets anxious with timed tests, social anxiety, and often has physical stress symptoms, such as headaches and gastrointestinal issues. May or may not be hyperactive.

CHAPTER 4

Fearfully and Wonderfully Made

How Parenting Kids with ADHD Can Reveal the Miraculous in Us All

S uddenly, Olivia was gone.

One second, she was with Carol (her mom) and her church youth group—laughing and soaking in the sights, sounds, and smells of a lively, music-filled plaza. The next second, she was swallowed up by a big crowd.

"Olivia!" Carol shouted. Then to herself, she mumbled, "Where is that kid of mine?"

The truth is, disappearing randomly was nothing new for Carol's fifteen-year-old daughter. Olivia's ADHD mind seemed to launch the teen on her own path, causing her to live in the moment, lost in her own world and caught up in her own timeframe. And all too often, Olivia was prone to sensation-seeking: She would jump into situations that many would label risky, and she'd do it without hesitation and without weighing the consequences.

Those realities sent Carol into motherly red alert.

Oh, Lord, I'm so scared for her, Carol prayed. *We took our eyes off Olivia for just one second, and now she's gone! She's not even answering her phone.*

Carol and Olivia were three thousand miles from home on a mission trip in San José, Costa Rica. Right from the beginning, the concerned mom had reservations about the trip. Olivia's sensation-seeking tendencies coupled with the dangers of Costa Rica's capital city made her question the wisdom of bringing her ADHD teenage daughter.

My girl is loving, Carol thought. *She just sees the best in people, which is why I thought this trip would be a good experience for her. Lord, please keep her safe. Please don't let anything bad to happen to my precious child.*

Carol stood helpless at the entrance of a tiny stucco church—the 12:30 p.m. rendezvous point. It was now 1:30. She stepped onto a sidewalk and looked left, then right. Directly in front of her was a crowded plaza—the center of the neighborhood. On each side were narrow, bustling streets that wove through a maze of ornate Colonial-era stone buildings. It was a postcard-perfect moment that had now become a terrifying scene.

"Don't worry, Miss Carol, we'll find her," insisted Libby, one of the student leaders. "She was last seen by two other girls a short time ago…just a few hundred yards from us. I'm sure she's safe."

Carol smiled and nodded in agreement. Inside, she was crumbling.

Leading a three-week mission trip in Costa Rica with a dozen enthusiastic teens and a handful of overwhelmed adult leaders was stressful enough. But now she had to rein in Olivia. Did she make a mistake by bringing her?

Carol and the high school youth group she led at her church in Missouri came to San José to help spruce up a struggling church and to lead a summer Vacation Bible School. That day was the big kick-off. Her teens were handing out flyers that promoted the event, and they were spending the day getting familiar with the neighborhoods near the worksite. Over the next fourteen days, most of the kids they'd encounter would come from very poor homes with very few opportunities. Carol challenged her students to break down walls that divided cultures and strive to build strong connections with the children. "This is a needy section of San José that could use a big dose of love," Carol told them. "Pour out your hearts—teaching, laughing, playing…and even crying with these kids. They need you."

Was Olivia getting it? Was she tuned in to the purpose of this trip? Could she contribute and help make a difference in the lives of the young people who lived there?

"Found her!" a voice yelled, snapping Carol back to reality.

"Oh, praise God . . . my prayers have been answered," Carol said.

A big grin stretched across Libby's face. "But you're not going to believe your eyes!"

"Uh-oh," Carol said. "Please tell me everything's okay!"

"Even better," Libby said. "Come take a look."

Carol and Libby caught up with Olivia one block away— halfway down a narrow ally that wove behind apartments and along a steep hillside. The teen was standing at the base of a rock wall, hurling paper airplanes upward to street kids sitting on top of the wall. The dozen or so children up top looked like a desperate bunch: shirtless adolescent boys with teardrop tattoos tripping down their faces; girls with hollow expressions; tiny munchkins with scruffy hair and tattered, soiled clothes.

Each time a boy or girl would catch one of the airplanes that drifted their way, the group would cheer and then toss them back to Olivia. In response, Olivia would comically jump, leap, spin around, and then launch the planes back toward the kids on the wall. All on her own, the teen had used her imagination and turned her stack of flyers into attention-getting toys.

"Incredible!" Carol said—her panic now turning to pride.

The mom felt as if she were watching a miracle unfold right before her eyes: her often unpredictable ADHD daughter, who didn't know a word of Spanish, was able to speak to the hearts of street kids. Olivia's actions were busting down barriers and bringing joy to a forgotten little alley in San José.

From Carol's perspective, her teen's out-of-the-box creative thinking led to some genius-level actions. She suddenly admired Olivia's boldness and her ability to "hyperfocus" on things that captivated her. In this case, she was determined to find a way to connect with neighborhood kids and get them excited about VBS.

Olivia looked up and caught her mom's gaze. "Oh—hi, Mom," she said matter-of-factly. "I found some kids who can come to church tomorrow."

"Yes, I can see that," Carol said, giving her daughter a hug. And then she whispered in her ear: "I'm so proud of you, but I was really scared, too. You left the group, and we couldn't find you."

"I'm sorry," Olivia said.

Carol bent down and picked up Olivia's Bible and a lone sheet of paper that lay on the ground. "Do you need this paper to make another airplane?"

"Not that one," Olivia said. "It's the letter you gave me before the trip. I read it, and I liked it: 'So, if God is for you, who can be against you?'"

Carol looked down and began reading the handwritten letter she had given Olivia...[1]

You Are a Masterpiece

So God created mankind in his own image,
in the image of God he created them;
male and female he created them.

(Genesis 1:27)

For we are God's handiwork, created in Christ Jesus to do good works, which God prepared in advance for us to do.

(Ephesians 2:10)

For you created my inmost being;
you knit me together in my mother's womb.
I praise you because I am fearfully and wonderfully made;
your works are wonderful,
I know that full well.

(Psalm 139:13–14)

Indeed, the very hairs of your head are all numbered. Don't be afraid; you are worth more than many sparrows.

(Luke 12:7)

He replied, "Because you have so little faith. Truly I tell you, if you have faith as small as a mustard seed, you can say to this mountain, 'Move from here to there,' and it will move. Nothing will be impossible for you."

(Matthew 17:20)

I can do all this through him who gives me strength.

(Philippians 4:13)

What, then, shall we say in response to these things? If God is for us, who can be against us?

(Romans 8:31)

All verses are taken from the New International Version.

Different Does Not Mean Defective

Having ADHD does not mean that a child has low intelligence, a lack of gifts or talent, or an inability to excel in life. It's quite the opposite, actually. And moms like Carol won't hesitate to point out the positives: "Kids with attention deficit disorder often demonstrate some amazing traits that can help them go far in life," she says.

Three key traits often define the ADHD mind:

Creativity: Children who have ADHD can be marvelously creative and imaginative. Because they consider a lot of options at once, they don't become set on one alternative early on and are therefore more open to different ideas. The child who daydreams and has ten different thoughts at once can become a master problem-solver, a fountain of ideas, or an inventive artist. Children with ADHD may be easily distracted, but sometimes they notice what others don't see.

Sensation-Seeking: Children with ADHD often have high levels of enthusiasm and spontaneity! They're interested in a lot of different things and have lively personalities. In short, if they're not exasperating you (and sometimes even when they are), they're a lot of fun to be with.

Hyperfocus: When kids with ADHD are motivated, they work or play hard and strive to succeed, displaying incredible energy and drive. It actually may be difficult to distract them from a task that interests them, especially if the activity is interactive or hands-on. Some children with ADHD exhibit hyperfocus: they can lock in with an exceptional degree of focus when they are interested in a task or a subject. But on the flipside, if you asked that same child to apply an equal degree of attention to a subject they don't find interesting, their mind would probably wander uncontrollably.

"The more I parent Olivia," Carol adds, "the more a masterpiece is unfolding before my eyes—and the more I see the miraculous in us all."

Carol encounters the miraculous everywhere she looks—on her and her daughter . . . even on strangers like you and me. And she's right.

> ## THE ADHD CHILD MAY EXHIBIT . . .
>
> ▶ Out-of-the-box, creative thinking
>
> ▶ A leaning toward sensation-seeking
>
> ▶ The ability to hyperfocus on subjects that interest them

Consider your body, for example. It is a marvelously created and complex machine. Inside are cells that build themselves from carefully designed and coded information, instructions that have been passed from one life to the next since their original inception.

Study your hands. One-fourth of all your bones are in this part of your body. With them, you can create the most delicate painting or lift heavy weights. And your very own fingerprints are uniquely yours.

Now think about your brain. It's so complicated that even the most advanced computer has nowhere near its efficiency. It not only controls your body, but with it you think, you create, you feel, you love, and—along with your spirit—you reach out to God.

Scientists' best guess is that the human body is built from about twenty thousand genes, and if you unspool all the DNA and take a look at what's inside, you're sure to find any number of differences from some imaginary normal.[2]

Some of us have noses that tilt a little to one side. Some of us have perfectly straight teeth without braces. We're tall, we're short, we're skinny, we're plump, we're every possible combination of those twenty thousand genes. And as you ponder the miracle of creation—especially how we're each "fearfully and wonderfully" made—the question is raised: Why are we so caught up with comparisons? Why do some believe we're inferior if we fall below a certain height and more acceptable if we tower above it? Why are kids who are diagnosed with ADHD so often viewed as different? Or even worse—defective?

It's because we pretend there's this thing called normal.

Yet as you explore the Scriptures, you'll notice that our Creator never defined what perfect DNA looks like, and He doesn't give us a definition of normal or defective. We know the things of Heaven are perfect, and that humankind's sinful nature warps everything below. But the idea that some of us are more or less perfect than others is completely false.

For you created my inmost being;

you knit me together in my mother's womb.
I praise you because I am fearfully and wonderfully
made;
your works are wonderful,
I know that full well.
My frame was not hidden from you
when I was made in the secret place,
when I was woven together in the depths of the earth.
Your eyes saw my unformed body;
all the days ordained for me were written in your
book
before one of them came to be.
(Psalm 139:13–16 NIV)

The configuration of body parts or the diagnosis of a neuro-developmental disorder shouldn't define who we are. We are already beautiful creatures made by a loving Creator. When He looks at us, He sees brokenness—because all of us are broken by sin—but He also sees completeness under the grace He wants to give us. There's no heavenly hierarchy of what we're given at birth. We're made how we're made for a reason.

Carol summed it up perfectly: "I see the miraculous in us all."

Let's move in for a closer look at the uniqueness of the ADHD brain.

ADHD and Creativity

Research shows that many individuals with ADHD are better able to engage in "out of the box" thinking, which is why they often exhibit startling originality.[3] Innovators, freethinkers, uninhibited risk-takers, hyperfocused geniuses—these are just a few of the labels ascribed to the ADHD mind.

LET'S GO DEEPER

UNDERSTANDING AND LOVING THE ADHD CHILD

In the remainder of this chapter, we will...

▶ Explore the many ways those with ADHD are able to think creatively

▶ Learn why some with ADHD are prone to sensation-seeking

▶ Discover how the ADHD mind is wired to hyperfocus

Nurture Their Creativity and Unlock Intuition

Creative thinking and intuitive inspiration have helped people of all ages to dream, innovate, and strive to make their mark on the world. Your ADHD child can too. They came into the world with the same potential as some of history's greatest minds: Leonardo da Vinci, Nicolaus Copernicus, Albert Einstein, Marie Curie, Jane Goodall, Jane Austen, Georgia O'Keeffe...the list goes on and on. Inventors and artists such as these developed techniques to call upon their genius minds to create completely new ideas and turn them into reality. According to Edward De Bono, one of the world's leading authorities in cognitive studies, we have two choices when it comes to thinking:

1. Thinking is a matter of intelligence. Intelligence is determined by the genes with which you were born.[4]
2. Thinking is a skill that can be improved by training, by practice, and through learning how to do it better. Thinking is no different from any other skill and we can get better at the skill of thinking if we have the will to do so.[5]

After reading Olivia's story, we hope you're inspired to help your ADHD child to dream big, to pursue change...and to never limit their thinking. Even if they don't feel smart enough or if they're bogged down by the countless unfair labels slapped on them, every child can change. Every boy and girl can improve and flourish—regardless of their IQ. As De Bono points out, every man, woman, and child can improve his life by improving his thinking skill.

Olivia has MIT- or Harvard-level potential, yet she was fooled by the labels people slapped on her. She believed all the lies she was told and was convinced she wouldn't amount to much. Thankfully, her mother knew differently.

And believe it or not, one of history's greatest minds under-stood this all too well.

At an early age, Albert Einstein had to shed false labels some ascribed to him.

Einstein's "Fanatic Freethinking"

Born in Ulm, Germany, on March 14, 1879, the young Einstein was a dreamy, curious individualist—not to mention a rebellious and often difficult student. According to his sister Maja, he loathed school, especially the German teaching system that was focused on rote learning. In fact, in her words, "an unsympathetic teacher at Munich's Luitpold Gymnasium told him that he would never get anywhere."[6] And as he grew into adulthood, Einstein was known to be "disorganized and forgetful"—he could never find his keys—and he was described as "someone who seemed oblivious to his surroundings."

Even his crazy hairstyle made an obvious statement: Einstein didn't fit in with the majority. He was a maverick, and he lived by his own rules. All this, of course, caused various medical experts to weigh in with their own explanations for his unconventional behavior. Some claimed that he struggled with ADHD, while others said he was dyslexic, possibly even autistic. Can any of these assumptions be true?

While historians can prove Einstein's genius and his contributions to science, they don't have concrete evidence that can link his constant inattention to neurological disorders. Yet according to Gail Saltz, M.D., Einstein's biography offers multiple opportunities to draw lines of correlation between his attentional difficulties—particularly in rigid academic settings—and his genius. Here's what she writes about Einstein in her book *The Power of Different*:

> By the age of twelve he threw himself wholeheartedly into mathematics. He spent one summer vacation plowing through his school's entire math curriculum, and also immersed himself in philosophy. He later described his voracious reading as "fanatic freethinking." In a way, that is highly familiar to anyone with ADHD—or to anyone who knows, treats, or teaches someone with ADHD—when Einstein was interested in something, he was completely enraptured, but when he was disengaged, nothing could encourage him to focus. His Greek professor at Munich's Luitpold Gymnasium told him in front of his entire class that he would never amount to anything. Later, his sister recalled that Einstein was considered lacking in intelligence when he was young....

Einstein was utterly unmotivated to apply himself to anything that he considered boring. Einstein found practical and earthbound subjects painfully uninteresting, so he simply ignored them. While his father wanted him to study engineering, Einstein chose the abstract subject of theoretical physics instead. He couldn't get excited about how to light up buildings, but he was enchanted with the essential nature of electromagnetism.[7]

Einstein was exceptional. Yet much of his story can be meaningfully applied to countless children and parents who must cope with the same erratic attention and roller-coaster performance that plagues kids with ADHD.

ˊ Unlocking the Genius Inside

Your child with ADHD can think like Leonardo da Vinci, William Shakespeare, and Albert Einstein. How? Let's explore a few of their secrets.

Be more curious like da Vinci. According to historians, there are two questions that da Vinci often asked himself: "What if?" and "Why?"

Asking "what if" requires our brain to project into the future, and it helps us see opportunities where we may have otherwise missed them; it helps us make connections, and it is a way to get our brain more goal-oriented. *What if I started a conversation with this person? What if I tried this new activity? What if I stopped being scared and started trusting more?*[8]

Also, encourage your child to ask "Why?" *Why is it important to have friends? Why is it important to be a good friend?* Instead of passively observing the world or going into automatic responses, we begin to question both our actions and other's motives. This line of questioning forces us to live more purposefully, just as da Vinci did. He refused to waste a second of his life. "How come?" helps us to use every second of our life with a mission.[9]

→ *How to Engage Your Child:*

This exercise is designed to get your kid thinking, processing deep ideas, making connections, and engaging in a conversation. It will also give you an opportunity to spark your child's curiosity and encourage "What if?" and "Why?" questions. As you work through this together, never ever shut down those "Why?" questions you probably hear a hundred times a day! Here's the plan:

(1) Pick a topic that's relevant to your child—for example, making a new friend.

(2) Turn that topic into "What if?" and "Why?" questions.

Example:

What if I talked to Jimmy during craft time and asked him if he'd like to come to my house for a play date?

What if he and I could end up becoming good friends?

Why is it sometimes hard to make new friends?

(3) Engage your child in a conversation, get them thinking, and then help them write down their responses.

What if_____

_____?

My thoughts: _____

_____

_____

_____

_____

_____

Why _____

_____?

My thoughts: _____

_____

_____

_____

_____

_____

Be more creative—like Shakespeare. While learning through memorization can be effective, William Shakespeare has shown us another equally important way of gaining knowledge: learning by heart. In other words, engaging the senses and the emotions as we learn. Shakespeare—like some of history's greatest creative minds —possessed three other qualities that set him apart:

He was an autodidact—he liked to teach himself rather than being spoon-fed information or knowledge in standard educational settings.

He was a polymath—someone interested in a wide range of subjects. Michelangelo and Leonardo da Vinci were prime examples, as well.

He was extremely persistent—even when confronted with skepticism or rejection.

Nancy C. Andreasen is a psychiatrist and neuroscientist who studies creativity extensively. She had the opportunity to scan the brains of thirteen of the most famous scientists, mathematicians, artists, and writers alive today. She also studied the structural and functional characteristics of their brains using neuroimaging. Here's an observation from that study: "Some people see things others cannot, and they are right, and we call them creative geniuses," she explains. "Some people see things others cannot, and they are wrong, and we call them mentally ill. And some people, like John Nash, are both."[10]

→ *How to Engage Your Child:*

Place several craft items on your kitchen table: finger paints, construction paper, glitter, crayons, clay—anything that will get your child's creative juices flowing. Set a timer and say, "Create a work of art for _____. Use your imagination and have fun!"

Einstein: Be more visual. In a landmark survey of the working methods of great scientists and mathematicians, Dr. Jacques Hadamard found that their thinking process was characterized not by language or standard mathematical symbols but by visual imagery.[11] This was clearly the case with Einstein, who participated in the survey. "The words of the language, as they are written or spoken, do not seem to play any role in my mechanisms of thought," he wrote, adding that his own processes instead "rely, more or less, on clear images of a visual and some of a muscular type."[12]

→ *How to Engage Your Child:*

Find a quiet and cozy place to be still. Have your child close his or her eyes and picture his or her favorite place. Take a little imaginary trip as you pretend that you are away on a long journey. Then describe how you feel when you finally return to your favorite place. Talk about your excitement, joy, relief, and peace. Then have your child do the same, describing in detail the images they conjure up.

ADHD and Sensation-Seeking

Every day when school let out for Gina's twelve-year-old son, Alex, she and her two best friends—Trish and Janna—got together at a nearby park. As they watched their children burn off energy on the swings and the slides, the ladies swapped stories and discussed current events. All three moms shared the same views on parenting, faith, and politics, and they each had the unique challenge of raising kids with ADHD.

Trish had three sons—ages eight, nine, and thirteen—and described them as being wildly different from each other. Her eldest boy was quiet and had an aptitude for the arts, the middle child was easygoing and very social, and the youngest was a competitive thrill seeker. Janna was busy with a seven-year-old son and an imaginative nine-year-old daughter, as well as a moody "tweenager" who was turning twelve in a few months. Gina had just the one son—Alex.

One day, Trish scooted next to Janna and Gina on a park bench and said, "Okay, I have a question: I desperately need to learn more about how an ADHD boy's mind works. I mean really, what in the world is going on up there?"

And with that, the three moms launched into a meaningful conversation about their unique parenting challenges—specifically, how to cope with an ADHD child's sensation-seeking. Let's listen in:

Trish: I'm seriously outnumbered by guys in my own home. There are days I wonder if I'm losing my mind. It's like they are in their own world, and sometimes it just doesn't make any sense.

Janna: It's all about "wrestle-ationships" in your house, isn't it? I've seen the broken furniture in your house, and you've seen it in mine. I'll never understand this guy-thing with wrestling all the time...and everywhere! But girls aren't any easier. Lately, my daughter has been so flighty and hyper—so I'm constantly talking her down from an emotional ledge. Her ADHD intensifies this behavior.

Gina: It's the same in my house. I'm always running interference for my son who risks life and limb on some new thrill of the day. He's a true blue sensation-seeker—and it's exhausting!

Trish: Every time I think I have my sons' ADHD tendencies figured out, something new pops up, and I feel clueless about what to do.

Janna: Yep. My daughter exasperates me, too. She sometimes plunges head-first into risky situations without thinking through the consequences. I'm learning from our therapist that there is a strong association between ADHD, risk-taking, and a lack of impulse control.

Gina: It's scary. But it's as if my son is happiest in a roller-coaster world, chasing one extreme adventure after another, rock climbing and white-water rafting in the summer and ice climbing in the winter. I don't mind the "safe" thrills. But I freak out when he wanders into dumb risks with his friends. I recently caught him and his buddies vaping in our basement. It's that kind of behavior that scares me.

Trish: Deep inside, he's a good kid. And you're an amazing mom—so involved and so supportive. He'll survive this, and I bet he'll grow up to be a firefighter or a rescue worker or something where he uses all that thrill-seeking for something good.

Gina: I hope so. But he's still so young and vulnerable. I'm so worried he'll get hurt.

Janna: It really helps talking about all this. I'm relieved knowing that I'm not the only one dealing with these constant fears. So—what can we do?

Gina: I guess we find a way to direct their scary risk-taking ways. We accept that it's real—just another part of the ADHD experience. We have to tackle it head-on and manage it.

Trish: Yep. We have to keep leading our kids. And it seems that supporting them has become more and more important. I need to find new ways to let them know that they can count on me when they get overwhelmed and confused.

Why Otherwise Sane Kids Do Crazy Things

It all comes down to the way children with ADHD develop neurologically.

In general, boys are the ones who are wired to be risk takers. As Dr. James Dobson points out in his book *Bringing Up Boys*, "one of the scariest aspects of raising boys is their tendency to risk life and limb for no good reason." Dobson cites a study that compares the risk-taking behaviors of boys and girls, concluding that females usually weigh the consequences and "are less likely to plunge ahead if there is any potential for injury."[13]

Yet interestingly, the ADHD brain (in both boys and girls) is often wired to move the child toward "sensation-seeking." In other words, many individuals with ADHD can easily discard inhibitions and can act impulsively. They are often drawn to thrill-seeking or excitement-seeking, and they possess the tendency to pursue new and different sensations, feelings, and experiences.[14] This trait describes people who chase novel, complex, and intense sensations; who love experience for its own sake; and who may take risks to pursue those experiences.

According to Northwestern University researchers, there's a genuine creative advantage to impulsivity.[15] Their study found that those with low impulse control have a stronger tendency to act on their creative urges rather than simply to think about them. In another study conducted at Ruhr University in Germany and published in *Child Neuropsychology*, researchers found that children with ADHD showed an enhanced ability to overcome "constraining influences." In other words, they could think outside the box.

What We Can Learn from Sensation-Seekers

According to Saltz, there is a strong association between ADHD, risk-taking, and lack of impulse control. "Imagine the person with ADHD as having a brain that's like a classroom," she explains. "Ideally there should be a teacher in charge who draws all eyes to her. In the ADHD brain, that authority figure is weak and inconsistent, and the children run amok. Not only does the child with ADHD have difficulty staying on task, he can have difficulty sitting still and thinking before speaking."[16]

Yet in spite of the challenges, sensation-seekers embody valuable attitudes and traits. The unique experiences they chase can cultivate joy, fulfillment, and coveted memories. New adventures provide an opportunity to grow and expand one's sense of self.

Thrill-seekers can be proactive and helpful in their communities. Many people plan and over-analyze how to respond to a situation, and the Bystander Effect demonstrates the tendency to shy away from unsettling circumstances. But thrill-seekers charge headlong into the fray and trust themselves to respond accordingly.

Navigating rocky terrain also instills confidence in one's ability to conquer future obstacles. Placing oneself in an unfamiliar or even perilous situation—learning to scuba dive or pilot a plane—pushes people out of their comfort zone, forces them to pay complete attention to a task, and instills confidence in their mind, body, and instincts.

"High sensation-seekers see potential stressors as challenges to be overcome rather than threats that might crush them," says Emory University psychologist and sensation-seeking expert Kenneth Carter. "This mindset is a buffer against the stress of life."[17]

ADHD and the Ability to Hyperfocus

Back home safe and sound from her mission trip to Costa Rica, Olivia turned her attention to a school science project, focusing every ounce of her energy on completing the assignment.

Scattered on her desk was a mishmash of various objects: a beaker filled with tap water, a dozen eggshells that had been cut in half and cleaned out, along with items that looked as if they'd be right at home in a science lab: borax, table salt, rock salt, sugar, baking soda, and several tiny bottles of bright food coloring.

She was creating eggshell geode crystals, and she'd been hard at work all evening. She didn't even hear the tap, tap, tap on her bedroom door. Her mom, Carol, poked her head in the room.

"Honey, I just wanted to say goodnight and—*wow*!" Carol stopped mid-sentence—both amazed by Olivia's impressive creations and a bit concerned about all the time her daughter was devoting to the science project.

She stepped into the bedroom and put her hand on Olivia's shoulder. Her teen was engrossed in her work, seemingly unaware that Carol was standing right next to her.

"Honey," Carol repeated, squeezing Olivia's arm. Olivia finally looked up.

"Hi," Carol said. "This is amazing, and you'll get an 'A' for sure. But it's getting late, and I'm concerned that you've neglected your other assignments."

"I've got to get this done," Olivia said. "And they're turning out even better than I thought they would. It's really been a fun experiment."

Olivia picked up a fragile orange geode creation. "This one's my favorite. Isn't it pretty?"

"Absolutely beautiful," Carol said. "Now when's this due?"

"Wednesday."

"And today's Sunday," Carol pointed out. "You've got an English paper that's due...when?"

"Tomorrow," Olivia said, her face turning red. "Okay, Mom, I'll stop doing this and start writing my paper."

Carol gave her daughter a hug and a wink and then left the room.

■ ■ ■

Hyperfocus, a common symptom of ADHD, is the ability to zero in intensely on an interesting project or activity for hours at a time. It is the opposite of distractibility, and it is common among both children and adults with attention deficit hyperactivity disorder.[18]

"When a child with ADHD is doing something she really enjoys, she may have a hard time stopping and turning her attention to something she doesn't enjoy as much," explains Nanette Gingery, a family therapist in Lincoln, Nebraska. "Medically speaking, hyperfocus is thought to result from low levels of dopamine, a neurotransmitter that is particularly active in the brain's frontal lobes. This deficiency can make it hard for a child with ADHD to shift gears and move on to other pursuits."[19]

Should a parent be concerned? Nanette says no, explaining that there's nothing inherently harmful about hyperfocus. In fact, it can be a very good quality. It enables some kids with ADHD to engage in freethinking and creativity, and they are better able to lock in and complete complex tasks— as we saw with Olivia in the story above. On the other hand, unrestrained intense focus can be a liability if left unchecked. Managing it is the key.

Four Ways to Harness Hyperfocus

1. Find ways to make schoolwork more fun for children
2. Allow a child to hyperfocus on something she enjoys as a reward for completing a task she doesn't find interesting
3. Set up external cues to redirect attention (i.e., a timer or an agreed-upon schedule)
4. Educate a child about how his brain works so he can learn to self-manage hyperfocus

PART TWO

LOVING YOUR CHILD

CHAPTER 5

Confidence Booster No. 1—Building Better Relationships

Here's How You Can Help Your ADHD Child Survive and Thrive Socially—from Handling Bullies to Unlocking Deeper Connections with Friends and Family

Bullying is abuse, not child's play, and too often, it's the kids with ADHD who feel the brunt of a put-down. Children can be cruel to their peers who stand out or who struggle with social skills. Here's a peek into the secret, painful world that is a reality for so many ADHD sufferers…

✉ *My teacher says I'm one of the smartest kids at my school, and that makes me feel really good. But my ADHD sometimes makes me act different than other kids—at least, that's what some of them tell me. There's this one girl who calls me "Zombie Girl" because I get real quiet sometimes, and I daydream a lot. She pulls pranks on me, and one of my best friends laughs and joins in with them. I want it all to stop, and I don't want to be different, but I don't know what to do.* (Emma, 10)

✉ *I've been told by my parents to pray for a bully. See, I get more than my share of bullying because I'm an ADHD kid. But my family and I believe in God and try to love everybody, even mean people—just as the Bible tells us to do. Recently, I gave it a try. During lunch at school, I caught up with this boy who has been teasing me. I sat right across from him and said, "Can I pray for you?" That caused all his friends to laugh, so he got up, grabbed me by the collar, and started dragging me toward the garbage can. In my head I thought,* I can't let this happen. *So I decked him. That was a bad, bad idea. He came right after me, and I ran, but he caught up and put me in the trash can. Then he punched me and said, "Hit me again and see what happens, you freak!" I was crushed. I tried to do something right, but it went wrong.* (James, 13)

✉ *I have a BIG problem with bullies. This one kid constantly picks on me, and he calls me "weird." What makes other kids hate me so much? My ADHD? It isn't my fault that I'm this way. That's what Mom and Dad tell me.* Pleeeeeeease, *can someone help me escape the torture?!* (Chad, 8)

✉ *A bunch of kids from my school have been bullying me online, and it really hurts. I know I'm not very popular or the prettiest girl. I'm a little overweight…and my mind works a little differently from other kids. I've been diagnosed with ADHD. But do I really deserve all this teasing?* (Isabella, 9)

■ ■ ■

Being a kid with ADHD isn't very easy, especially when it comes to navigating the brutal social landscape. And as a parent, you can't help but wonder if your child's impulsive behavior puts a giant bullseye on his back, making him the target of ridicule. Sometimes kids with ADHD draw negative attention to themselves: They talk out of turn or blurt inappropriate remarks at the wrong moment; they miss social cues and annoy classmates with their heightened energy; they latch onto a new friend, practically smothering them. All this puts them at a greater risk of being bullied.

That's how it was for nine-year-old Melody.

She was a budding pianist who had dreams of one day becoming a famous musician. Maybe she would compose great songs and see her name in lights on Broadway. Maybe she would one day perform at the Kennedy Center in Washington, D.C. The problem was most of her peers didn't see much greatness in her.

"Why are you so weird?" a classmate once asked her during craft time at school. "What happened to you?"

"I bet her mom dropped her on her head," another girl remarked, causing other kids around the table to laugh.

Melody just shut down, unsure of how to handle the painful remarks. And in the days and weeks that followed, she was pelted with more scarring word bullets: "clumsy," "stupid," "ugly."

Despite having a high IQ and an aptitude for music—and so much promise for the future—Melody began to believe the names other kids were calling her. She couldn't stop thinking that she had brought on the bullying because she was different...because she had ADHD. Like a pressure-cooker, anger began to heat up inside.

"Honey, what's going on?" her mother, Rae, asked her one evening when she walked into the living room and watched her daughter pound the piano keys with her fists, tears rolling down her cheeks. "Talk to me. What's making you so sad?"

Melody couldn't quite get the words out. All she could do at that moment was beat the air with clenched fists and groan.

A couple of phone calls to Melody's teachers and a few of her neighbors, and Rae slowly began to piece together the facts and make sense of the random words Melody was using to describe herself. The whole painful scenario was now becoming clear to Rae: Not only was her daughter the victim of teasing and torment at school, she desperately needed help managing key relationships—with other kids, with adults in her life, and even on the home front.

Something's got to change, Rae told herself. *But where do I begin? How can I squash the cycle of bullying and equip my kid with social skills that can help her throughout her life?*

■ ■ ■

Boys and girls just like Melody must survive a hostile world that consists of bullies and their victims; one in which the strong prey upon the weak.

We know kids with ADHD who feel trapped in a prison of loneliness and shame—children who, in spite of feeling terrified, hide their pain behind emotionless masks, never flinching and always fearing humiliation from their peers. Deep down they're miserable.

How about your child?

Maybe they're a victim. Maybe they've even begun to think that they have to hurt others in order to avoid being a target. Regardless, like so many other kids, some begin to think they are powerless and that the only answer is to shut up and put up with the pain. In the words of Rae, "Something's got to change."

The best way to help an ADHD child improve social skills involves parental intervention on multiple fronts: addressing

LET'S GO DEEPER

UNDERSTANDING AND LOVING THE ADHD CHILD

In the remainder of this chapter, we will ...

▶ Learn how you can equip your child to handle bullies

▶ Discover ways you can help your child make and keep friends their age

▶ Explore tips on helping your child talk to other kids

diet and exercise, managing medical issues, getting involved at school, and getting your child engaged in some form of behavior therapy (more on this later in the chapter). In turn, as these interventions improve a child's life, they can have a ripple effect of diffusing taunts and teasing and strengthening relationships. So what specific things can a parent do? Teach your child to read social cues, tune in the feelings of others, interpret behavior, and respond appropriately. Yep—that's a tall order for anyone, especially a child! But as you step into the role of "social coach," you'll observe positive change.

When Your Child Is the Target of Bullying

Talking it out is the first step toward helping your child find relief. While it's hard and even embarrassing for most kids to admit they're being bullied, it can be even more challenging for a kid with ADHD to process and verbalize their emotions. The most important thing you can do is help them understand three key messages: (1) they are not alone, (2) they have your support, and (3) things are going to get better.

Start by saying something like this: "You don't have to keep this stuff in; that's not fair to you. And if you know of someone who is being bullied—or if you are the one being picked on—go to a teacher or the principal. It's not snitching; it's helping a classmate. It also shows real courage. We're going to solve this together."

As you open the door to a conversation about bullying, here are some practical ways you can help your child. Obviously, you will need to adapt these ideas to fit your child's age and maturity level.

Discover what triggered the bullying. Ask some basic questions: "What were you doing right before the bully started picking on you?" "What did you say?" "What can you do differently to avoid being teased?" The goal is to help your child figure out what caught a bully's attention and what provoked the incident. For example, was your kid talking excessively? Did they make a negative remark that the other child misunderstood? Maybe they blurted out something inappropriate or were too clingy and overly affectionate. Avoid blaming your kid for their part, and assure them that you are on their side. Emphasize that bullying is never okay.

Teach them how to distinguish bullying from joking. Talk to your child about the difference between bullying abuse and playful joking. Share examples of "friendly teasing" in which your child is in on the joke. Teach them how to laugh at themselves in a nonthreatening situation. Kids with a sense of humor are less likely to be bullied than are kids who take everything to heart.

Employ these strategies to shut down bullying:[1]

- Teach older children to use humor to diffuse a situation.
- Tell them to agree with the bully, that is, if the bully's remark is silly or innocent: "Yeah, my hair is messy today. I've never learned to use a comb!"
- Answer back with a slightly exasperated tone. Say, "Oh really? Whatever!" And then move on.
- Avoid the bully if you don't have a comeback ready.
- Call them out on their remark. Ask, "Why did you say that?"

Help them avoid danger. Encourage them to defuse a situation with a direct, calm answer: "Look, I don't have a problem with you...so I'm going now." And then walk away. Leaving the scene instead of standing there arguing from the top of their lungs is the safest way to maintain peace.

Find hope through God's Word. Regardless of your family's faith experience, there's great wisdom in the Bible, not to mention some common-sense guidance that can help your child steer clear of a bully. So if another kid has targeted your child for no apparent reason, here's what Scripture says they should do:

- Proverbs 22:3: "The prudent see danger and take refuge, but the simple keep going and pay the penalty." (NIV)
- Proverbs 15:1: "A kind answer soothes angry feelings, but harsh words stir them up." (CEV)
- Romans 12:17–18: "Don't pay back evil with evil. Be careful to do what everyone thinks is right. If possible, live in peace with everyone. Do that as much as you can." (NIRV)

Improving Peer Relationships

Rae groaned inside as she watched Melody fumble her way through a social setting. They were both at a friend's birthday party, and Melody was trying hard to fit in. Way too hard.

"I'm Melody," she said loudly, standing a bit too close to a girl she had just met. And then she reached out and tugged on the stranger's T-shirt. "I like your Dr. Seuss shirt. Those are my favorite stories, too."

The girl pulled away and squinted, her eyes scanning Melody from top to bottom.

Melody moved in even closer. "Hey, wanna play a game or do something together?"

It practically broke Rae's heart as she watched the girl back away even more and then leave the room, totally snubbing Melody. Her daughter stood awkwardly alone in an otherwise crowded room—rightfully disappointed, not to mention clueless as to why she was being rejected.

But Rae seized a perfect teaching opportunity: "I'm so proud of you for talking to that girl and trying to make a new friend," she whispered to her daughter privately. "That took courage, and you said some good things. It was nice that you gave her a compliment. But here's what you can do differently next time ..."

Do conversations like these happen frequently with your child? If so, you're not alone, and you're headed in the right direction. Research shows that children with ADHD tend to be extremely poor monitors of their own social behavior.[2] They often do not have a clear understanding or awareness of social situations and the reactions they provoke in others. As Rae and so many other parents often observe, ADHD can prevent their kids from accurately assessing or "reading" a social situation. That's why it's so important for parents to step in and teach their kids the social skills they need.

"It's hard for anyone—young and old alike—to master the art of reading people," Rae admits. "But for kids like Melody, it's a really, really big challenge. So, I'm trying to nudge her in the right direction by pointing out things like observing personal space and lowering our voices when we get excited. So far she's listening—and it's starting to make a difference."

Kids need other kids in their lives just as adults need other adults. At our core, every one of us is relational, so having positive peer friendships is important regardless of our age. Unfortunately, many kids with ADHD have a hard time making and keeping friends and finding acceptance among their peers. The impulsiveness, hyperactivity, and inattention associated with ADHD can wreak havoc on a child's attempts to connect with others in positive ways.[3]

Yet not being accepted by one's peer group, feeling isolated, different, unlikeable, and alone—this is perhaps the most painful aspect of ADHD-related impairments, and these experiences carry long-lasting effects.[4] Though kids with ADHD desperately want to make friends and be liked by the group, they often just don't know how. This is where a parent's role as "social coach" is critical. You can boost your child's confidence and help him experience positive change by showing him how to improve his social skills.

Here are some additional steps you can take:

Guide Them through the Unspoken Rules of Relationships

Children with ADHD tend to have a hard time learning from past experiences. They often react without thinking through consequences.[5] One way to help your child is to do what Rae did: Provide immediate and frequent feedback about social blunders and inappropriate behaviors.

Teach them how to "read" other people. Role-playing is a useful way to drive home a point. As you act out and model appropriate behavior, help your child practice positive social skills as well as ways to respond to challenging situations like teasing.

Teach them how to start and maintain a conversation. It's very important for them to learn how to do these three key things: (1) take a breath, (2) listen when another person is talking, and (3) ask about the other child's ideas or feelings. Explain that taking turns in a conversation is the right thing to do. Say this: "It helps if you show interest in the other child."

Teach them appropriate behaviors in social settings. This includes negotiating and resolving conflicts as they arise, sharing, maintaining personal space, and even speaking in a normal tone of voice that isn't too loud.[6] Practice these prosocial skills again and again and again. Shape positive behaviors with immediate rewards.

Give Them Opportunities to Make Friends

For preschool and elementary school children, play dates provide a wonderful opportunity for parents to coach and model positive peer interactions for their child and for the child to practice these new skills.[7] Set up these playtimes between your child and one or two friends at a time rather than a large group. Structure the playtime so that your child can be most successful.

As a child gets older, peer relationships and friendships often become more complicated, but it is equally important for you to continue to be involved and to facilitate positive peer interactions. The middle school and high school years can be brutal for a child who struggles socially. Even if a child remains unaccepted by the peer group at large, having at least one good friend during these years can often protect her from the full-on negative effects of ostracism by the group.

Research and get involved in groups in your community that foster positive peer relationships and social skills development like Boy Scouts, Indian Guides, Girl Scouts, Girls on the Run, sports teams, etc.[8] Make sure the group leaders or coaches are familiar with ADHD and can create a supportive and positive environment for learning prosocial skills.[9]

Communicate with the school, coaches, and neighborhood parents so you know what is going on with your child and with whom your child is spending time. A child's peer group and its characteristics have a strong influence on the individuals within the group.

Get Your School On Board

Once children are labeled "different" by their peer group because of a mental disorder, it's nearly impossible to shed this reputation. In fact, being singled out as different is perhaps one of the biggest challenges your child may have to overcome socially.

Studies have found that the negative peer status of children with ADHD is often already established by early-to-middle elementary school years, and this reputation can stick with the child even as he or she begins to make positive changes in social skills.[10] That's why it's critical that you work with your child's teachers, coaches, and school administrators to get their help with damage control, as well as finding ways to boost your child's self-confidence.

Young children often look to their teacher when forming social preferences about their peers. A teacher's warmth, patience, acceptance, and gentle redirection can serve as a model for the peer group and have some effect on a child's social status.[11]

When a child has experienced failures in the classroom, it becomes more and more important for the child's teacher to consciously find ways to draw positive attention to that child.[12] One way to do this is to assign the child special tasks and responsibilities in the presence of the other children in the classroom.

Make sure these are responsibilities in which your child can experience success and develop better feelings of self-worth and acceptance within the classroom. Doing this also provides opportunities for the peer group to view your child in a positive light and may help to stop the group process of peer rejection. Pairing the child up with a compassionate "buddy" within the classroom can also help facilitate social acceptance.

Friendship Basics

Help them to choose more face-to-face time with their friends...and limit game time and other activities online. (1) This keeps them from becoming addicted to their favorite pastimes, and (2) it reduces the chances of getting into trouble in their high-tech hangouts (for example, cyber bullying).

Help them choose friends, not phonies. Tell them this: "It's important to have friends—guys and girls to hang out with, to share great experiences with, to laugh with. But sometimes friendships aren't always smooth sailing, so we must choose our friends carefully." Explain that true friends don't laugh at our imperfections. Instead, they accept us just the way we are, they stay by our side through thick and thin, they stick up for us...and they can be trusted. A phony, on the other hand, constantly puts us down, tries to turn us into something we're not, takes off when the going gets rough, lies to our faces, and stabs us in the back.

Help them choose friends who are positive influences. Say this: "The people we hang out with can have a big impact on our lives. We can't fool ourselves. Bad friends can destroy us. But good ones build us up."

Help Them Make and Keep Friends

Teach them these friendship basics…

Start with a smile. Being friendly is important, and a smile can enable your child to communicate acceptance without saying a word. Though it seems like kindness doesn't always come easy for kids, they'll be surprised at how many friends they can make—and keep—by being understanding and putting others at ease with a smile and a little kindness.

Risk reaching out. A kid named Dillon mustered up the courage to make a new friend in his classroom at school. He started talking to a new kid, and they really hit it off. Now they're good friends. The truth is, most kids are going through the same kinds of things—the same pressures and fears. And they all pretty much want the same things: friends. Encourage your child to reach out and say, "Hi!"

Communicate. That's how friendship grows. Tell your child this: "Nothing strengthens a friendship more than two people sharing their thoughts and feelings with each other. Talking and connecting allows us to know and to understand one another." So it's a good idea for them to watch those put-downs. Joking around is one thing, but constantly hurling insults or laughing at people's mistakes can really hurt. If words can be weapons, they also can bring healing.

Say you're sorry. Tell your child that if they've wronged someone, they need to take responsibility and own up to the mistake. It's hard, but it's the first important step toward mending a broken friendship.

Six Great Conversation Starters

- Sports: Your child can talk about their favorite pro teams, amazing plays, sports you participate in—anything!
- Animals: People love to talk about their four-legged friends. "Do you have a pet?" "What's its name?" "How long have you had it?"
- Embarrassing moments: We all love to laugh, especially at ourselves. Pull stories from the "I-Was-So-Embarrassed Files" of your life.
- Faith: Here's a big part of a child's life that they can share. Encourage them to talk about what's going on in children's group at church, camps, great things God is doing in their life, and so on.
- Vacations: There's so much to talk about—traveling, dream vacations, adventure trips...crazy places they've visited. Tell them to be creative: "Let's say

your parents offered to take you and a friend anywhere you want to go in the world next summer.
What kind of vacation would you choose?"

CHAPTER 6

Confidence Booster No. 2—Balancing Structure with Spontaneity

Daily Routines Coupled with Freeform Thinking Can Help Kids Stay Focused

Ethan and Sydney burst into their Sunday School class and instantly raced to their favorite teacher, Ms. Gina, both wrapping their arms around her.

"Ah, my favorite eight-year-old boy named Ethan and my favorite eight-year-old girl named Sydney," Gina said with an enthusiastic singsong tone.

"We're the only Ethan and Sydney in the class," Ethan pointed out.

"You're right," Gina said. "Now you know what to do."

The twins reached into a toy box and pulled out a Thomas the Train set with intricate tracks, buildings, and railcars, and instantly went to work piecing everything together on the floor. As other students filed into the classroom, they were greeted with equal enthusiasm, but these kids took their seats at a long rectangular table.

Sondra, the twins' mother, seemed to swell with joy as she watched from the doorway. She moved closer to Gina and whispered in her ear: "Thank you for the special care you give Ethan and Sydney. I wish all their teachers shared your empathy."

Gina, in her usual humble manner, awkwardly received the praise, turning the attention back to the needs of the kids. "Oh, thank you," she said. "I believe that structure balanced with a whole lot of spontaneity goes a long way—especially with kids prone to distraction. If I keep their hands busy, their minds will tune in—often in most miraculous ways."

The Structure–Freedom Balancing Act

Most people don't have the patience for kids like Ethan and Sydney. Ethan is disruptive, randomly blurting out inappropriate remarks, and he just can't stop moving and tapping his pencil even after his teachers ask him a million times to stop. Sydney, on the other hand, is constantly off daydreaming in her own world, distant and removed from the rest of her peers.

Ms. Gina is a rare teacher. And she has found a key to reaching, teaching, and motivating children with ADHD: Keep their hands busy, and their minds will tune in.

In other words, balance structure with spontaneity.

Building a Healthy Structure

No doubt about it, children with ADHD need guidance, compassion, and understanding from their parents and teachers as they navigate the path of dealing with their condition. Like most mental health disorders, ADHD is not black and white. It is a perplexing condition that can affect the academic and social lives of children who have it, possibly into adulthood.[1]

You've likely heard how important it is to expose such children to routines and a structured environment. But what does that mean exactly, and how does structure help? Structure is a term one hears a great deal about as it relates

LET'S GO DEEPER

UNDERSTANDING AND LOVING THE ADHD CHILD

In the remainder of this chapter, we will . . .

▶ Explore tips and ideas on how to build healthy structure

▶ Find your child's rhythm

▶ Learn tips for getting them engaged

to parenting children with ADHD. So, what does structure look like? Simply put, a structured environment is one that is organized and predictable.

When your children have day-to-day routines and a schedule to follow, this creates structure in their lives. Consistent house rules, expectations, and consequences that your child clearly understands (and which you positively reinforce) help maintain a predictable environment. That way, your child knows what to expect. This knowledge creates a sense of security, which is why most children benefit from structure whether they have ADHD or not.[2]

Many children are capable of structuring their chores, schedules, and activities, and of developing good habits on their own. For a child with ADHD, however, this is a much more difficult undertaking because of how the disorder functions.

Children with ADHD struggle with the ability to regulate themselves. This means they find it challenging to stop impulsive behaviors and keep their focus when there are so many distractions pulling them in different directions.[3]

The symptoms of ADHD lead to problems with self-control. As a result, children with ADHD need more external controls (i.e., structure) in order to help them manage symptoms. When you build in external controls at home, you are helping your child to experience more successes, and you are teaching them good skills and habits that will serve them well.

With structure, children learn to set aside the same block of time to complete their homework or to establish a bedtime and morning routine. Simple moves such as taking a shower and picking out clothing for school the night before can make getting to school on time the following morning much easier. The routines, reminders, and limits you set and the consistency you provide is a lot like the scaffolding used on tall buildings. This scaffolding provides support as the building is going up, or "growing."

Similarly, when you create structure at home, you are providing the support needed to help your child be successful and develop greater competence. As a result, your child's self-confidence grows. Eventually, this will help him develop skills to organize and structure his life as he moves into adulthood.

Healthy routines do not happen overnight. Here are some tips to help you create a healthy structure that will help your child grow and learn to be on time.

Create a list of tasks that your child can do on his own. If the tasks are too overwhelming, your expectations will have opposite results. If the list is created with the child's abilities in mind, it can be an amazing tool.

Have your child help you create the list. Talking through the goals and how to accomplish them will help your child comprehend why the list of tasks exists.

Be realistic. Nothing is more discouraging than a to-do list that is not possible to complete. Start small, and let your child grow into more responsibility. If you think a task should take five minutes to complete, give it ten minutes instead. Then, if it is done early, it is time to celebrate.

Group the tasks into smaller segments. If you want to teach your child how to keep the house clean, for example, create a list of the tasks for each room and post them in a prominent place in that room. For example, you can place the kitchen list on the refrigerator. The bathroom list can be on the mirror over the sink. And the bedroom list can go on his wall or door. Smaller lists are easier to understand and accomplish.

Plan some down time. Creative free time can boost a child's imagination and spirit. Stepping away from chores to play and rest can be fun for both child and parent.

Be specific. List specific items that need to be kept in specific places. If your directions are too vague, your child might interpret them differently, leading to frustration. Be consistent with your directions. Routines are hard to establish if they change too often.

Praise your child's accomplishments. Daily words of encouragement should be a part of your routine. Positive actions deserve positive affirmation. Be sure to recognize his efforts as well as his accomplishments.

Collaborate, Don't Dictate

Some children are naturally organized and embrace the routines of life, but most don't. As a parent, it is your responsibility to assess your child's personality and create a routine and lifestyle that fits. If you are introducing structure to a child who is not naturally attracted to organized routines, it may be challenging at first. Creating a safe and positive environment for the child is a vital element when introducing these life skills. This process can be begun by simply talking with your child. Be honest and hopeful as you express your goals and expectations. Inviting him into the brainstorming process will help you accomplish these goals together.

It's okay to express your feelings in a respectful way. It is also okay for your child to be allowed to express her feelings in the same respectful way. You may use different words or examples, but it is the honesty of emotions that creates a safe environment for everyone involved. A child's vocabulary is not as large or well developed as an adult's. He or she may become frustrated and act out, or withdraw and become quiet. It's okay to take it slow. This type of healthy communication often takes some time to develop.

Use examples to explain concepts that may be too large for a child to comprehend. You could say, "I'm concerned that if we don't come up with a laundry routine, your clothes won't get cleaned and you will have to wear dirty clothes to school." This shows that you care for his well-being and are trying to create a routine for his benefit. This example shows the positive outcome of the routine and the opposite negative outcome if one is not developed. Allow time for your child to ask questions and explore the many different outcomes of following or not following a routine. This will help him to incorporate the desired routine into his own world through his own understanding. This type of ownership will help him to embrace the daily schedule instead of resisting it.

Brainstorm together as you design the schedule. Discuss your expectations as you identify the tasks your child is to accomplish independently. Younger children will need more help, especially in the beginning. Over time, and with repetition, they will become more comfortable working without constant supervision. Again, it's okay to take it slow. Even when it's necessary to make changes to a routine, it is best to incorporate those changes over several days.

Kid Time versus Adult Time

Children see their world very differently than adults do. Their perspective is usually more immediate and is focused on the moment they are in, whereas most adults have developed the skill of planning ahead and shaping their actions to benefit their future. Thinking beyond the current moment is a skill that can be developed with a little practice over a period of time. This is one of the possible long-term benefits of a daily routine. This is an important aspect to consider when creating a daily schedule. Keep in mind that the longer the task, the more likely a younger child will struggle to complete it. "No child is going to be able to sustain focus unless the work is segmented into smaller chunks."[4]

The Pomodoro technique is based on the concept that people are more motivated to complete a task if there is a specific time given to work. Research shows that the ideal time for adults is approximately twenty-five minutes. This includes a five-minute break for every twenty-five minutes of work. And there should not be more than four Pomodoros in a row. Beyond this, the motivation drops, and the productivity levels decrease.

The effective time for younger people, in middle and high school, is similar to adults but decreases after three Pomodoros. A child's attention span is usually connected to his age. So it is important to assess your child's ability to focus on a task and create a schedule accordingly. Don't stress out. Over time, your child's ability to focus on a specific task will change, which will require adjustments to the schedule. Stay in tune with his progress and adapt to his ever-growing abilities.

Find Your Child's Rhythm

Are you a morning person? Do you jump out of bed ready to take on the world? Is your mind flowing with creative ideas the moment you open your eyes? Or does it take you a few hours to truly wake up and wrap your head around your goals for the day? Maybe you are an evening person. You may be wide awake at 11:00 p.m. while everyone else is going to bed. We all have a rhythm. As adults, we discover our personal rhythm through the years and adapt our daily schedule accordingly. Sometimes, we do this naturally as we select a career, lifestyle, and social life. Other times, we are challenged to match our natural rhythm to the demands of our day.

A child also has a personal rhythm. Some kids may be running around full of life and energy at 6:00 a.m. while their parents are trying to sneak in another hit on the snooze button. Other children may struggle just to walk upright for the first few hours of the day. The major difference between the rhythms of adults and children is that the adults have had several years to identify their rhythm and make adjustments while kids have not. They are most likely unaware that they even have a rhythm. And if they are aware of it, they lack the maturity and experience to construct their own schedule to accommodate that personal rhythm.

One of the most useful steps you as a parent can take is to observe your child's natural life rhythm and create a daily schedule that works for them instead of against them. For example, if your child is a morning person, choose the harder chores or academic subjects for the morning hours. If your child's energy levels are low in mid-afternoon, then schedule some downtime to match. This can be challenging if a child's rhythm is opposite from yours. There are times when the two will not align. Not all schedules and activities will easily match up with a child's natural rhythms. But with a little observation and some adaptation, building a daily schedule around a child's natural rhythm can be beneficial. It's at least a good place to start.

Task by Task

Sometimes it's hard to sit still for long periods of time. This is especially true for young kids. One of the best ways to keep them engaged is to break their daily routine into smaller activities throughout the day. Designate different physical spaces, or stations, for each task. This combination of shorter segments of time and a variety of locations can be a winning strategy to keep your child engaged.

For Younger Children: Adopt the Montessori approach when you set up your activity stations. Each location should be equipped for the task. A reading corner should be comfortable, with a variety of age-appropriate books. A science station can include safe hands-on items to help a child experiment with how things work. A play station should include some of their favorite toys that can be easily stored in containers.

Encourage your child to have fun moving from station to station. A burst of physical activity between stations can help a child focus on a new task. For example, they can hop, roll, or dance as they move to a new station. Once they arrive, set a timer and challenge them to focus on that station's activity until the buzzer sounds.

For Tweens and Teens: A variety of stations also works for older children. Try to avoid placing stations in their bedrooms if possible. Again, each station should be equipped for the assigned task. Older kids can set their own timer and move from station to station by themselves. More than likely, the older the child, the less likely they will want to hop, roll, or dance from activity to activity. Their down time will also look a little different than a younger child's. Legos may be replaced with screen time. Video games may take the place of race cars. Interacting with friends on social media has become a driving force in the life of teens. As a parent, it is important to set the parameters for these activities in advance.

Kids Need Kids

Kids need social interaction. Younger kids need to play with each other and older kids need to "hang out." This can be one of the benefits for children who attend school outside of the home. But just because they go to school doesn't mean that this need is being met. So whether your child goes to brick-and-mortar school or homeschools, it is important for him to spend time with his peers. Joining a sports team, learning to play chess, taking a baking class, scheduling a play date at the park, or going to the movies are a few ways for your child to interact with other kids who have the same interests. If an in-person gathering is not possible, there are a variety of ways to interact online. From study groups to gaming to story time, encourage your children to interact with other kids their age.

Tips for Keeping Them Engaged[5]

1. Seat the student away from doors and windows that may distract him or her. The student may work best closest to the teacher.

2. Allow physical activity breaks (stretching) and incorporate movement activities into a lesson. If possible, allow for outdoor instruction time.

3. When possible, provide academic instruction to these students with ADHD in the morning. Evidence suggests that on-task behaviors of a student with ADHD worsen over the course of a day.

4. Write important information down where the student can easily reference it, most likely at their desk.

5. Divide large assignments into small segments. Write these segments down. Have the student cross the items off as they are completed.

6. Provide frequent breaks for the student to get a drink or walk around the room.

7. Allow the student with ADHD to run errands for you (taking a note to the office, for example)

or put him in charge of sharpening the classroom pencils.

8. Provide the student with a stress ball or other object to play with discreetly at their seat, especially when she needs a break.

9. Write the schedule of the day on the student's desk and allow him or her to cross off each item as it is completed.

10. Recognize and praise aloud all good behaviors. Be specific about what the student is doing correctly.

11. Provide an assignment book for the student to keep track of homework and daily work. Encourage parents to sign it so they know what is going on in the classroom. Communicate with the parents as much as possible.

12. Form small groups for students with ADHD to work in so as not to get distracted and lost in a large group.

13. Allow the student with ADHD to work in a quiet zone within the classroom. This should be a place in the room that is quiet and free from visual stimulation.

14. Establish a secret signal with the student to use as a reminder when he or she is off task.

15. When giving directions, make eye contact with the student and be as brief as possible.

16. Use visuals. Highlight words in colored chalk or bright ink. Underline and circle important things to remember.

17. Use auditory cues. Set a timer and encourage the student to work uninterrupted until the timer goes off. Allow the student a break following the work period.

18. Provide specific, well-defined rules for the student with ADHD. Write these rules down and tape them to the student's desk. These rules should have clear consequences.

CHAPTER 7

Confidence Booster No. 3—Harnessing Their Daydreams

Fuel Their Imaginations and Put Their Creativity to Work

Bart Simpson is the ultimate underachiever. He's content with average performance, his mind is focused on instant gratification, he doesn't count the cost of his actions, and he wastes energy concocting elaborate schemes for dodging responsibilities.

And when it comes to goals, his head is definitely in the ozone: "I'd like to be the first human to ever skateboard on Mars. Cowabunga, dude!"

Unmotivated. Unfocused. Unrealistic. Sound familiar? Unfortunately, way too many people think that Bart's world describes the planet occupied by kids with ADHD.

Take twelve-year-old Alex, for example. (He's Olivia's younger brother and Carol's son.) He was just a few weeks away from experiencing a milestone in his life, his thirteenth birthday, but Alex didn't feel like celebrating. He was flunking out of school, and he had even gotten into some trouble when was caught vaping with other kids at his school.

Yet his mom was determined to help Alex turn things around.

During a weekend camping trip, Carol asked Alex, "What do you hope to accomplish during your lifetime?"

"I want to be a marine biologist," he responded, "or maybe a photographer."

"Great!" she said. "Now how do you think you can achieve these goals?"

"Humph!" Alex grunted as he shrugged his shoulders and poked a stick in the campfire. "You know I'm not doing too well in school, and I don't own a camera. I dunno. But each summer when we visit relatives in Florida, I love snapping pictures at the beach and visiting the aquarium. Working with sea animals would be cool."

Two weeks later, after Alex had blown out the candles on his birthday cake and had unwrapped most of his gifts— mostly practical things the boy found boring, like socks and T-shirts—Carol plopped a big package on her boy's lap.

"There's one last gift to open," she said. "We saved the best for last. Go on—open it up and see what's inside!"

"No, Mom, maybe later," Alex protested. "I just want to go back to my room and be alone. Everything's all wrong this year."

Carol lifted an eyebrow. "I'd say things are pretty right," she said.

Alex shook his head and groaned, embarrassed by all the eyes staring at him. Carol continued talking.

"Look around you," she said. "Look at where you live and consider the food you get to eat. Some people in the world don't have any of these things. And think about all these people in this room who love you. We're not perfect, and we each have our share of struggles, but we're a family. A strong family. And we look out for each other."

Secretly, Alex was tracking with everything his mom was saying, but a mixture of pride and embarrassment wouldn't allow him to admit it. Instead, he glanced at the package on his lap and gently began tugging at the ribbon. When the last piece of wrapping paper fell to the floor, the gift was revealed.

Alex looked up and gasped. "Mom, Dad—you can't afford this!"

"We're the gift-givers here, so we'll decide what we can and can't afford."

Carol and her husband had practically emptied their savings account on a present that Alex had talked endlessly about for years yet had always thought was out of reach: a 35mm camera, along with various lenses.

"Every budding photographer needs a good camera, right?" Carol said.

Alex sat speechless, feeling as if he was holding more than just a camera—it was as if he held some sort of link to his future in his hands. "This is amazing!" he said as he fiddled with it.

"There's a carrying bag in the box, too," Carol pointed out. "I figure it will come in handy the next time you're in Florida, photographing those beautiful beaches."

A grin stretched across Alex's face. "Mom, Dad…you're both pretty amazing. What would we do without you? Who would we be?"

Suddenly, Alex's thirteenth birthday didn't seem so empty. And from that moment on, he began to see his parents differently. From that moment on, his world began to make a lot more sense to him.

During that milestone birthday, Alex unwrapped the greatest gift a kid could ever receive. Of course, it wasn't an expensive camera. It was the gift only a nurturing parent can give: hope.

■ ■ ■

Inside Alex is a future Jacques Cousteau or an Ansel Adams. He really is bursting with potential. The problem is that his distractibility and impulsivity (caused by ADHD) were putting up roadblocks in his life. Without the proper spark from his parents, he could end up stuck in mediocrity—always dreaming, but never doing.

How about that boy or girl in your life? Are they floundering or flourishing? The keys to motivating them center around these crucial steps:

Fuel their imaginations. Get them excited about the future and all the possibilities ahead of them: the things they can experience, the places they can one day go...the very special people they are inside. Encourage them to dream big and to explore a few possibilities right now. (For older children, this could mean taking photography lessons, volunteering at the local zoo, joining the band, or going out for a sport.)

Help them live beyond the moment. It's not unlike Alex to squander the day playing video games at the expense of tomorrow's big exam. Help your child manage distractibility and help her set in motion good habits. Show him how today's choices can impact tomorrow's opportunities. Encourage her to begin setting realistic goals.

Build their self-esteem. Perhaps they have been emotionally slammed on the court or in the classroom. Perhaps they feel trapped by labels slapped on them and the lie that they'll never amount to much. Help them to see that their life is like

---

LET'S GO DEEPER

UNDERSTANDING AND LOVING THE ADHD CHILD

In the remainder of this chapter, we will...

▶ Discover ways to spark their imaginations

▶ Learn how to unleash their creativity

▶ Set a plan that can help launch their dreams

---

a work of art that's still in process. Tell them that God would never say, "This is who you are—and who you'll always be." Instead, Jesus says, "Just imagine what you can become."

Put Their Creativity to Work

For some kids, the symptoms of ADHD might foster creativity. Yet these same challenges can keep them from translating their ideas into reality. As we've discussed, children with ADHD often struggle with planning, time management, and following through on tasks.

For example, a child with ADHD might be bubbling with ideas for a short story for creative writing class. But they might not remember the ideas long enough to write them down.

A teacher might say a child's science fair project has lots of promise. But that child might not be able to get together a list of materials required to build it, let alone start the project or complete it on time.

There are many ways to help kids express that creativity, though. The first step is to recognize a child's creativity and see it as a strength.[1] It's also important for kids with ADHD to work on the skills that could keep their creative dreams from becoming a reality, like organization and time management. Improving these skills can help clear the way for creativity to flourish.[2]

Creativity helps children solve problems, gives them an artistic outlet, and makes life fun. So let's get practical. Here are some tips on how parents can nurture creativity in children. The key is giving time, space, and freedom to kids with ADHD (especially middle-schoolers) to do what they want to do without criticism. That works wonders for their confidence. Downtime gets their dopamine flowing, not only through the thinking parts of the brain but the reward centers as well. It may be the only time of the day that they feel comfortable in their skin.[3]

For kids with ADHD, any pressure to achieve can cause tension and discouragement. They are especially sensitive to criticism. It takes a lot of positive responses to counteract one negative response. And it's hard for them to get positive responses when day-to-day tasks seem boring, they are struggling to meet other people's goals, or are discouraged from thinking outside the box.

Nurturing Free Thinking and Creativity

Allow a kid with ADHD to be spontaneous during craft time, and you'll be amazed by his creativity. Most work best when they are given the freedom to tinker, explore, and create. And according to current research, the benefits are life-changing.

The title of a recent documentary film, *I Remember Better When I Paint*, sums up the findings of a growing body of research into the cognitive effects of making art. The movie demonstrates how drawing and painting stimulates memories in people with dementia and enables them to reconnect with the world. Yet people with dementia aren't the only beneficiaries. Studies have shown that expressing themselves through art can help people with depression, anxiety, or cancer.[4] And doing so has been linked to improved memory, reasoning, and resilience.

Here's how parents can help their kids tap into the power of creativity.

Give them plenty of time to work. It's no secret that kids with ADHD have an abundance of creativity just looking for an outlet.[5] And it's important that parents give their children plenty of time to do nothing. This is good for a child's mental health.

Parenting experts, psychologists, educators, and even neuroscientists are expressing public concern that children today lack true downtime. Some see the modern child as overscheduled by ambitious parents, shuttled from high-pressure sports practice to tutoring to cultural-enrichment activities.[6]

Give them their own creative space. Creativity is usually messy. Set aside part of a basement or garage for your child's projects. Or give the kitchen over to him for an afternoon.[7]

Give them the tools and materials they'll need. Help your child assemble a mini-junkyard—things like duct tape, wire hangers, round oatmeal boxes, shoeboxes and Styrofoam packing, cardboard tubes, scraps of fabric or wood, things with parts missing, old wheels from a toy. Other raw materials are paper, pens, and markers.[8]

Access to tools goes along with a selection of materials. A good gift for a middle-schooler is a basic toolbox. You can never have too many scissors, staples, metal rulers, or screwdrivers. Drop your old sheets, shower curtains, and shirts into the junkyard for messy activities.

Give them free reign. Once equipped, don't tie your child's hands or mind with rules and directions. Forego critiques, unless safety requires otherwise. One thirteen-year-old we know told her mom she wanted to make a dress. The mother gave her some remnants, needles, and thread, and let her try.

When a parent shows confidence in his middle schooler's choices and encourages her to follow her own plan or whim, that confidence is contagious. She learns that her choices are sometimes right, that her personality is okay, and that it is fine to do things because they feel right, even if they don't serve someone else's purpose.

Sparking Creativity in Young Children (up to Age Six)

Children this age love to play with anything and everything. They may reconfigure and recombine toys to suit their play, using and enjoying them differently than the manufacturer intended![9]

Parents must allow this combination, even though they might prefer to keep toys organized and sorted. For example…

- Let them mash play-dough in a sandbox to make "breaded patties"
- Encourage them to make gondola cars out of Lego blocks, sticking roll after roll of tape across the kitchen counters

It's best to use open-ended, unstructured play materials. Such toys have no one right way of being played with, they offer excellent play value, and they spur the imagination and inspire creativity.[10]

Sparking Creativity in Older Children (Ages Six to Twelve)

These are the creative years! Children in this age range carry on imaginative play throughout the day at home, at school, and during play dates. They play "house" with friends, create a theater using puppets, or pretend to be pirates, aliens, or superheroes. They play with household items and construction materials.

Here's a tip: Don't pack up or give away creative materials such as dress-up trunks or arts and crafts items under the assumption that children already have such things or better substitutes at school. That's not always the case. Parents often prefer the neatness of screens and controllers over having paint splashed on their rugs, and who can blame them? But it is important to keep a range of creative play items accessible to children and keep adding to them until about age thirteen when they start leaving behind their physical toys.[11]

Sparking Creativity in Teens

No doubt about it, a teen's world today is way different from the one we grew up in. Our kids are plugged in, and it sometimes feels as if their computers and cell phones have become extensions of their bodies.

The internet is an amazing megalopolis of cyber-circuitry with unparalleled benefits in communication, and currently more than 251 million North Americans are connected.[12] At the same time, your child is just a click away from trouble. In addition to all the good stuff online, the internet contains a gushing cyber-sewer of bad stuff that has invaded way too many homes.

Our advice: Redeem technology in your household. Help your teens tap into their creative sides through their online encounters. It's a place where they can do art projects, compose music, and write. They can be very creative using a different medium, somewhat like how painters are different from sculpture artists. In addition, computer games like Minecraft are based on creative play. You can research some options online. We recommend thoroughly investigating games before you make them available to your children, however, as some have chat features that can leave your children vulnerable to predators. Enough Is Enough is one organization specializing in internet safety that contains a wealth of information for parents on its website. For a sampling, visit https://internet-safety101.org/videgameinfo.

CREATIVE KID CONNECTIONS

Games and Exercises Designed to Spark Their Imaginations

Game #1: Illuminate My Steps

Save this activity for evening. When it's dark outside, click off the lights and turn on a flashlight. Have each family member grab someone's hand and go for a journey around the house. Carefully navigate your way around furniture, down hallways, up and down stairs—occasionally clicking your flashlight on and off. Eventually arrive at your destination: your bedroom. Climb into bed (assuming it's big enough). Reach into a "treasure bag" (or box) that you placed there earlier, and pull out some snacks, maybe even some drinks. With the lights still out—and the flashlight on—launch into creative conversation.

- How did this flashlight help us get to our destination?
- What happened when I turned off the light?
- What other things in life help to illuminate our steps?

Game #2: My King of Kings

This activity is especially suited for young children. Using gold-colored poster board or purple and yellow construction paper, help them create a "King of Kings" crown. Encourage them to color it, and then decorate the royal headpiece with sequins, glitter, and other shiny treasures. In addition to the crown, help them make hats for a cast of other characters in your make-believe castle: a queen, a prince and a princess, brave knights, even a crazy court jester. Next, pick a chair that will serve as your throne, and gather some old coats and shawls that the kids can use as robes and formal wear. When the stage is set, have everyone pull on a costume and take part in a magical celebration. Let them take turns ruling the party as king. End with a reading. (Choose your favorite story about kings and their kingdoms.)

- What does a king do?
- How important is it for a king to be good?
- What do you think the ultimate kingdom—Heaven—will be like?

Game #3: Building Courage

Before you meet, pull out three large bowls and fill each one with different items: place cooked spaghetti in one bowl, Jell-O in another, and gummy worm candies in the third. Next, place the bowls in brown paper sacks. Dare your kids to come forward, put on a blindfold and—without seeing what's inside—bravely stick one hand in each bag to feel the items. Add to the drama and ham it up. Make up a story: Tell everyone that you just returned from the meat department at the supermarket and asked the butcher to let you take home some "spare parts." Say something like: "Who has the courage to relinquish their hand to my mystery bags?" Have them describe the experience and try to guess what's inside. And then turn the conversation to the subject of courage.

- What went through your mind as you touched each item?
- Did you have to muster up courage? Why or why not? (Have them explain their answers.)
- Describe those moments in your life when you need extra courage.

Game #4: Caring for Others

Go shopping with your child. Together, pick out items that you can give to a homeless shelter or donate to a church food drive: socks, undergarments, canned foods, toiletries, etc. Go together as you hand over these items to the charity of your choice.

- Why is it important to help others?
- What are some creative things we can do to meet others' needs?

Game #5: Fighting Temptation

Play a game of "Pass or Tell." On separate slips of paper, make a list of several different scenarios that include temptations. For example, "You are in a store and your friend wants you to steal a bag of chips. What do you do?" Place the slips of paper in a hat. Have each person pull out a scenario and read it out loud. Then that person must answer how she would handle the situation. You can even include some of the times you have been tempted in life.

- Is everyone tempted?
- If so, how often?
- How can certain temptations harm us?

Launch Their Dreams

Pause for a moment and think about your child. *Who is this kid? What abilities has he or she been blessed with?* Now think of ways that you can nurture those talents and help launch his dreams. Keep in mind that nurturing the abilities of your child doesn't mean fitting him or her into your ideal image of who you think they should be. Help your boy or girl to discover their unique, God-given talents and experience them to the fullest. This exercise can help.

Step 1: Encourage Your Child to Dream

Take a look at your child's gifts and life dreams. Think about his or her interests, desires, and the kinds of things they'd like to pursue in life. Ask some questions:

- How would you describe yourself?
- What would you like to be when you grow up?
- Who is your greatest hero?
- Who would you like to be like?
- Now share some of your dreams. If you could be anything right now, meet anyone, go anywhere, and do anything…who, what, and where would that be?

Step 2: Pinpoint Your Child's Personality

My kid is often described as (circle only one pair of words and phrases):

"Mechanically Minded" / Technical

Inventive/ "Problem-Solver"

Creative / Artistic

"Outdoor Enthusiast" / Adventurous

Athletic / Competitive

Scientific / Mathematical

Investigative / "Fact-Finder"

"Legal-Minded" / Detail-Oriented

"People Person" / Communicator

Planner / Organizer

Step 3: Zero In on What Helps Your Child Learn

Respond to the following statements.

Ways my child learns and grows best include:

- Hands-on experiences
- Storytelling
- Learning in a group setting
- Learning by themselves
- Building and creating things
- Through music and art

- Through science and technology
- Using a computer

Other things that help my child grow include:

1.
2.
3.

Things that block growth include:

1.
2.
3.

My child's top *ten* sources of inspiration include (list people, books, movies, talks, journeys, service projects, mission trips, etc.):

1.
2.
3.
4.

5.

6.

7.

8.

9.

10.

My child's strengths include:

My child's weaknesses include:

Key ways in which my child makes friends include:

1.

2.

3.

4.

5.

Step 4: Help Your Child Set Some Goals

Teach them this:

1. Goals for a thriving life are similar to goals in sports. We strive to attain them. There's joy in achieving them. We long to execute them again. Don't be afraid of setting some goals for your life.

2. There are three things we must remember about setting and achieving goals: they are concrete, measurable, and attainable.

A concrete goal is one we can put into words.

A vague desire to "do better in my English studies" is not very concrete. But "improve grammar, punctuation, and writing" is a solid goal. Goals are most concrete when written down.

A measurable goal is one that allows us to see progress.

"Know the Bible from cover to cover" is tough to measure. But "read the New Testament this summer" allows us to mark your progress with that little ribbon in your Bible.

An attainable goal is one that can reasonably be completed.

"Make friends with everyone I meet" is both concrete and measurable, but it's hardly attainable. "Make three new friends at school this year" is a goal that meets all three criteria.

CHAPTER 8

Confidence Booster No. 4—Launching a Better Tomorrow

Strong Parent–Kid Connections + Heartfelt Discipline = a Promising Future

Marie wasn't about to give up on her thirteen-year-old son, Jamal.

Despite tension between them—and some hurtful things he'd said—Jamal was a good kid. Marie knew he was struggling with the worst year of his life: His father had died unexpectedly ten months earlier, which had broken both Marie's and Jamal's hearts.

"Honey, you haven't touched your spaghetti," she said to her son during dinner. "You've got to eat—otherwise you'll get sick."

Jamal shot a hurt look at Marie. "Too late, Mother," the boy snapped. "I'm already sick—sick of all the crud I deal with every day. Totally sick of my life!"

"Then you don't have to eat," Marie said. "Let's talk. I'll listen. Tell me what's going on today—"

"Why'd Dad have to die?" Jamal asked.

"I wish I had an answer, but it's one of those terrible things that I just don't understand either—"

"It isn't fair!" Jamal snapped, interrupting Marie. "He shouldn't have died. Now it's just you and me, but we're not a real family. Everything is so messed up. I just can't take it anymore."

Before Marie could utter another word, Jamal stood up and threw his fork on the table. "Look, I don't want to talk—to anyone." With that, he stormed out of the kitchen.

Marie slumped back in her chair and pushed her food away. Jamal was on an emotional roller coaster, which was completely understandable after all he'd been through. But mix in the boy's struggles with ADHD, and Marie felt as if she had a ticking time bomb on her hands. The weary mom was scared, confused, and desperate. Most of all, she was starting to lose her patience.

As she sat at the kitchen table, she began to think about a promise she had read in the Bible:

Do not fear, for I have redeemed you;
I have summoned you by name; you are mine.

When you pass through the waters,
I will be with you;
and when you pass through the rivers,
they will not sweep over you.
When you walk through the fire,
you will not be burned;
the flames will not set you ablaze.
For I am the LORD your God,
the Holy One of Israel, your Savior....
(Isaiah 43:1b–3a NIV)

Marie rubbed her eyes and took a deep breath. *I'm barely treading water, yet I know I've got to trust. I realize I have to stay strong for Jamal.*

Later that evening, Marie stood quietly by her son's room and poured out her heart in prayer: *Lord, I know Jamal doesn't mean to act this way. And I know that I need to be a source of strength—and reach out now more than ever. Please be my source of strength. Give me the right words and actions. Most of all, don't let me lose him.*

Marie tapped on the door. "Jamal, can I come in?"

"Whatever."

Marie pushed open the door. "I just wanted to say good-night...and maybe get a hug."

Jamal just blinked.

Marie sat down on the edge of the bed and embraced her son.

■ ■ ■

From a pandemic that resulted in loss for so many families to struggling communities reeling with economic uncertainty, life is hard these days. And for households dealing with the added challenges of mental disorders like ADHD, tensions are at an all-time high.

In spite of our circumstances, how is it possible for a houseful of people to love each other so much—yet at times feel so disconnected from them?

Why is it that we can live under the same roof with our spouses, sons, and daughters, be so close to them—which means we know all of their strange quirks—yet sometimes feel like complete strangers to each other?

The answer is obvious: an emotional war has erupted between many parents and their kids. It's that "war of independence," a perfectly normal part of growing up. With each step, the child in your life moves farther down a path to independence, steadily breaking free from Mom and Dad. This process takes on an extra layer of concern and challenge for the parent of an ADHD child. So understanding and loving them takes on even greater importance. It is essential that we diffuse the

tension so many kids are feeling, draw closer to them, and
do all we can to guide them
into a better tomorrow.

Improving Parent–Kid Relationships

As a parent, you set the
stage for your child's emotional and physical health,
and you have control over
many of the factors that
can positively influence the
symptoms of your child's
disorder. And guess what?

> ## LET'S GO DEEPER
>
> ## UNDERSTANDING AND LOVING THE ADHD CHILD
>
> In the remainder of this chapter, we will...
>
> ▶ Strengthen parent–kid connections
>
> ▶ Examine strategies for more heartfelt, empathetic discipline
>
> ▶ Discover how to nurture peace on the home front
>
> ▶ Clear up communication barriers

Your kids want a deeper connection with you. They need
to hear, "I love you," "I'm proud of you," and "I won't
give up on you."

They need you to be there for them. Most of all, they need
you to guide them through their roller-coaster emotions and
the everyday ups and downs of living with ADHD.

As we've pointed out through these pages, many children
with ADHD are stressed and anxious. And far too many feel

constant pressure; now, more than ever, they need change. They long to be accepted by their peers, but most importantly—whether they admit it or not—they hunger for family support and connection. They're counting on you to teach them, protect them, and look after their well-being in this often-frightening world. They need you to equip them to navigate life. Here's how you can nurture a deeper relationship with your child: Get connected with three basic relational links—keys that can unlock the door to your child's world.

The first relational link is empathy. Through the years, we've talked to children and families from all walks of life and from nearly every corner of the world. The kids we meet often echo the same message to parents: "Take an interest in how my world looks and feels . . . and try to understand what I'm going through." This is especially the yearning of kids with ADHD—even if they're not always able to put this desire into words.

As we pointed out at the beginning of this chapter, they must navigate an often-brutal landscape that's characterized by loneliness and peer fear.

The second relational link is trust. "I need this from my parents more than anything else," a teenage boy told us. "I can't handle it when they think I'm doing drugs or getting into trouble when in reality I'm not. I need them to trust that I'm a good kid—even if I stumble."

Now listen to the ache of another older boy who is struggling to respect his parents: "It's hard to trust my parents when they tell me all these things I can't do that I see them doing every day. How can I listen to them?"

Trust is fragile and is sometimes hard to build, yet it's universally important to every boy and girl. It's also a primary reason older children and teens may shut you down while other adults—such as coaches, youth ministers, or teachers—can command their full attention.

"It hurts when Mom and Dad don't have time for me," a nine-year-old told us. "But it hurts more when they say no all the time and don't let me do stuff with a friend. I don't like it when they don't trust me."

The third relational link: consistent, balanced connections. This means both setting parameters and knowing when to step back. It means picking your battles and letting go from time to time. Above all, it means taking an interest in your kid's world every day and letting them step into yours.

"I want to be closer with my parents," says another child we met. "I need to hear from them, 'I love you.' I need to know that they are proud of me—and that they don't think I'm weird because I have ADHD."

Face it: kids are stressed out. Far too many feel the constant pressure to prove themselves in classrooms, on playing fields, and especially among their friends. As they move through the elementary years and into adolescence and ultimately adulthood, they need you to help boost their confidence. It will grow as they experience a deeper relationship with you.

Eight Great Ways to Improve Home-Front Connections

Set the tone with a positive attitude. When you're stressed, they're more likely to be stressed as well. The best way to help your child meet the challenges of ADHD is to model a positive attitude. This comes a little easier as you strive to keep things in perspective. Remind yourself that your child's behavior is often related to a disorder and that it isn't always deliberate. Hold on to your sense of humor. What's embarrassing today may be a funny family story ten years—or even ten minutes—from now.

Try to keep a sense of humor and nurture a sense of hope. Sometimes, the keys to success in treatment are persistence and humor. Call someone who will listen to the bad news but will also lift your spirits. And keep reminding yourself of the positive aspects of ADHD—such as energy, creativity, and intuition. Remember that many, many people with ADHD do very well in life.[1]

Don't sweat the small stuff and be willing to make some compromises.[2] One chore left undone isn't a big deal when your child has completed two others plus the day's homework. If you are a perfectionist, you will not only be constantly dissatisfied, but you will also create impossible expectations for your child.

Believe in your child. Think about or make a written list of everything that is positive, valuable, and unique about him or her. Trust that your child can learn, change, mature, and succeed. Reaffirm this trust on a daily basis as you brush your teeth or make your coffee.

A child who senses his parents' resentment—and pessimism about his prospects—is unlikely to develop the self-esteem and can-do spirit he'll need in order to become a happy, well-adjusted adult. For a child to feel accepted and supported, he needs to feel that his parents have confidence in his abilities. Once parents learn to look at the gifts of ADHD—things like exceptional energy, creativity, and interpersonal skills—they can see the shine inside their child.

You, too, can see the "shine" in your children with ADHD. They are destined for something wonderful, something that would be impossible for those calmer, regular-energy-level children. I can think of several occupations where boundless energy would be an incredible asset. I'm even jealous of the tireless enthusiasm for life the child with ADHD has and wonder what more I could accomplish if I were so blessed. Do your best to love your child unconditionally. Treat him as if he were already the person you would like him to be. That will help him become that person.

Make it clear that ADHD isn't a choice. It isn't an excuse for irresponsible behavior or laziness that can be controlled, and it touches everybody in the family in a daily, significant way. Let each member of the family become a part of the solution since each has been involved with the problem.[3] Educate your household. Many problems will take care of themselves if all family members know the facts about attention deficit disorder and understand what's going on. Listen to everyone's questions, and make sure they all get answered. The more they know, the more helpful they will be.

Balance attention within the family. The attention may be negative, but the child with ADHD often gets more than his share—and that means the others often get less. This imbalance creates resentments among siblings and deprives them of what they need. Siblings need a chance to voice their own concerns, worries, resentments, and fears. They need to be allowed to get angry as well as to help out.

When you have one-on-one time with your child, talk about just them. Focus on that child, not on yourself. If you do so, you might be able to get them to open up. It might take patience and persistence, but it can happen. If your relationship is estranged because you belittled or criticized your child, the last thing you want to do is criticize. Get yourself out of the way and completely look at that child; talk to them about what they're interested in. Your child looks up to you. If they see you as a real parent and a leader, then they will be able to see that ADHD and leadership qualities can go together and that they can make a difference in this world. A lot of good can come out of that.

Find positive solutions when tensions arise. Give everyone a chance to be heard. ADHD affects everyone in the family, but it affects some silently. Let those who are in silence speak. Get the whole family involved, pointing them toward positive goals rather than negative outcomes. Applaud and encourage success. One of the most difficult tasks for ADHD families is getting onto a positive track. But once this is done, the results can be fantastic. A good therapist or coach can help.

Set clear expectations. All family members need to know what is expected of them, what the rules are, and what the consequences are. Target the problem areas and brainstorm solutions. Typical problem areas are study time, mornings, bedtime, dinnertime, times of transition (leaving the house and the like), and vacations. Once these are identified, everyone can approach problems more constructively. Negotiate how to make it better. Ask one another for specific suggestions, and brainstorm solutions together. Approach problems as a team.

Build a strong team. Consistency helps, so try to present a united front. The less that either parent can be manipulated, the better. Develop as much support as possible. From pediatrician to family doctor to therapist, from support groups to professional organizations to national conventions, from friends to relatives to teachers and schools, make use of whatever supports you can find. Group support can help you solve problems and keep your perspective.[4]

Teach them to count the cost. Help them see that actions have consequences and that these are not always fair. Help your child think about how a choice now might impact his or her plans, family, or future. Ask, "Will a choice you face put you in physical danger? Will you risk emotional damage? Is momentary acceptance from a peer worth destroying your future?"

Strategies for Heartfelt Discipline

You've tried to remain calm, attempting to reason with them. You've even turned up the volume: raising your voice, lecturing, threatening, giving time-outs, taking away toys and privileges, canceling outings, bribing, begging, and even spanking—yet you're still at your wit's end. What discipline strategies work best with kids with ADHD?

First, take a deep breath and remind yourself of two parenting truths:

ADHD is the problem, not our kids.

Never punish them for negative behavior that's outside their control.[5]

Next, take to heart the relational links we discussed at the beginning of this chapter. Be determined to do everything in your power to advocate for your child's emotional and educational needs. Help them sort through the bad news that constantly bombards them and move toward a better, more hopeful tomorrow.

Think about all the negative labels that may have been slapped on your child: "unruly," "lazy," "hyper," "disrespectful," "out of control," "slow," "spacey," "weird." Kids who repeatedly hear bad things about themselves eventually come to believe them. Regardless of how frustrating your child's behavior can be, refrain from adding to the negative remarks.

"While it's true that your child's mind works differently, he certainly has the ability to learn and succeed just like any other kid," explains George DuPaul, a professor of school psychology at Lehigh University in Bethlehem, Pennsylvania.[6] "Look at it this way—if your child was diabetic or had asthma, would you, for one single minute, hesitate to advocate for his benefit? Just as a diabetic needs insulin and an asthmatic child needs help breathing, a child with ADHD needs their learning environment regulated."[7]

So, let's get back to our original question: What discipline strategies work best for kids with ADHD? Answer: Heartfelt, empathy-based discipline. Follow these essential steps.

Separate Discipline from Punishment

When Ethan threw his toy truck into a blazing campfire—even after repeated warnings to move back from the fire and not play too close to it—immediate, swift punishment was in order. Not only did his mom Sondra give the eight-year-old a swat on his backside and a stern talking to about his safety, she also sent him to his tent for the rest of the evening.

On the other hand, Ethan's twin sister Sydney had received praise earlier that evening when she stopped interrupting her brother during campfire story time. She even took turns roasting hot dogs with him.

"Sydney, you did a good job taking turns and sharing with Ethan," Sondra said. A short time-out earlier had corrected the problem, and positive feedback reinforced a valuable lesson.

While some parents misuse the terms discipline and punishment—too often getting them mixed up—the fact is that each involves a different approach. As Sondra demonstrated, discipline involves a teaching moment, and it's all about guiding a child toward good behavior. It includes an explanation of the bad behavior and a redirection to what's acceptable—along with positive reinforcement each time the child makes a good choice.

The word "discipline" literally has its roots in the Latin word *disciplinare*, to teach or train. Parents need to teach their children good behavior; it doesn't just happen.[8] And it is incredibly hard work, especially because when children act badly, it can get on a parent's last nerve and trigger an angry response, like yelling or spanking.

Punishment, on the other hand, uses fear and immediate, swift action to force a child to behave. It certainly has its place as we parent our kids, but it should never involve physical or verbal abuse, and it's best reserved as an extreme measure. For example, Ethan endangered his life when he got too close to the campfire, and he made a bad choice by throwing his toy into it. Immediate intervention was required at that moment.

Often, the best way to discipline a child with ADHD is through a simple program of behavior modification: Define age-appropriate, attainable goals, and then systematically reward each small achievement until the behavior becomes routine.[9] Rewarding positive behavior rather than punishing negative behavior enables children to feel successful, and it motivates them to make good choices in the future.

Don't Punish Behavior That's Out of Their Control

When Carol's fifteen-year-old daughter Olivia disappears randomly—as she did during their mission trip to Costa Rica—Carol intervenes promptly with appropriate discipline to protect her child, but is careful never to punish behavior that's out of Olivia's control. Carol knows that Olivia's ADHD mind seems to launch her on her own path, causing her to live in the moment, lost in her own world and caught up in her own timeframe.

Carol weighs each of these behaviors as she guides, teaches, and disciplines her daughter. She knows that distractibility is a common symptom of ADHD—something that Olivia is often unable to control.

Repeatedly punishing her daughter for behavior Carol knows Olivia can't control could set the teen up for failure. Eventually, Olivia's motivation would disappear too, and the parent–child relationship would suffer as well.

Punishment is the right course of action when a child's life is endangered and when it's clear that he or she is being defiant—for example, if Olivia had deliberately disappeared out of anger. But in most cases, Carol tries to give her the benefit of the doubt, consistently nudging Olivia in the right direction and reminding her of family parameters and expectations.

Strive to Reward Positive Behavior

Say things like, "I love it when you…" or "That was so nice that you did that!" or "Because you behaved so well today, let's read an extra story tonight." Children like praise and may be more likely to behave well when they see that it's worth their while.[10] And it's a refreshing change from what most kids with ADHD are used to hearing.

These lively children feel they're constantly being told, "No—what you are doing, thinking, and feeling is wrong. Don't do that, sit down, calm down, be quiet."

In a parent's quest to quash negative behaviors, many of us overlook all the positive ways in which our children behave. Therefore, we must retrain ourselves to look at the positives. As we observe our kids being good and doing things well, we must encourage and praise them. This teaches them to do what we want them to do, not what we want them to stop doing. And most important of all, rewarding positive behavior is crucial for a child's self-confidence.

According to Claire McCarthy, M.D.—senior faculty editor at Harvard Health Publishing—all it really takes is positive feedback from one supportive, nurturing relationship to make a difference in a child's life. "This gives children a buffer and helps them know that they aren't alone and that they matter to someone," she writes on her Harvard Medical School blog.[11] "While all parents want to have a good relationship with their child, the demands of daily life can get in the way. Try to spend regular time with your child when they have your undivided attention. Ask about their day, get involved in activities they enjoy, spend time doing things together. Make sure your child knows that no matter what, you have their back—and you will love them."[12]

Research backs up the power of positive feedback. Current studies show that having five positive interactions to every negative interaction best supports and sustains constructive student–teacher relationships.[13] It can work at home, too.

It's known as the 5-to-1 ratio, and here's the thinking behind it: positive feedback nurtures a child's well-being, improves feelings of connectedness, helps build resilience, and plays a part in helping grow and maintain healthy relationships.

Positive interactions may include friendly conversations, specific praise or positive feedback, and nonverbal acknowledgment. Negative interactions may include criticism and reprimands.

With the 5-to-1 ratio, kids can improve academic engagement and reduce classroom disruptions, simply because the classroom has a more positive climate. And creating positive interactions in the classroom helps students invest in the value and purpose of classroom instruction. Students have a stronger sense of belonging and feel more connected to their teachers, which naturally leads to improved behavior and engagement. When students feel connected and have a sense of belonging, they're naturally more motivated to achieve.

Make happiness and laughter the cornerstones of family life. Spend fun time with your children. Go with them on bike rides. Play with them at the park. Visit museums together. Take them to the movies. Sure, life with ADHD can be challenging. But the rewards are great for parents who really connect with their children.

Set the Example

Parents are a child's most influential role model, so think carefully about your behavior. If you're unable to control yourself, how can you expect your child to exercise self-control?

It's perfectly normal to feel angry at your child from time to time. It's not okay to continually shout at her. You wouldn't dream of screaming and swearing at friends or coworkers, so you know you can control your anger if you must.

Next time your child does something that causes your blood to boil, leave the room, take a few deep breaths, or do something else to calm yourself.[14] When you demonstrate self-calming techniques in this way, you teach your child the importance of managing her emotions.[15]

If you do lose your temper, do not hesitate to apologize to your child.

Take Care of Yourself

As your child's role model and most important source of strength, it is vital that you live a healthy life. If you are over-tired or have simply run out of patience, you risk losing sight of the structure and support you have so carefully set up for your child with ADHD.

Seek support. One of the most important things to remember in rearing a child with ADHD is that you don't have to do it alone. Talk to your child's doctors, therapists, and teachers. Join an organized support group for parents of children with ADHD. These groups offer a forum for giving and receiving advice and provide a safe place to vent feelings and share experiences.

Take breaks. Friends and family can be wonderful about offering to babysit, but you may feel guilty about leaving your child, or even about leaving the volunteer with a child with ADHD. Next time, accept the offer and discuss honestly how best to handle your child.

Take care of yourself. Eat right, exercise, and find ways to reduce stress, whether it means taking a nightly bath or practicing morning meditation. If you do get sick, acknowledge it and get help.[16]

Navigating Storms on the Home Front

Let's continue to explore effective parenting solutions—this time, learning how to navigate the daily storms that inevitably wage war on the home front. When it comes to the specific needs of kids with ADHD, what can you do to cool down the hot spots and restore peace? Here are some ideas:

Allow for a cooling-off period. Unless you detect some serious disrespect, a little bit of the "cold-shoulder treatment" from your child won't hurt. True, it doesn't feel too good, but your child needs a chance to cool off and to process the situation. (For that matter, you need to cool off as well.) Give them time to cool off, but...

Don't let them shut down for too long. Too much of the cold-shoulder treatment means that you could end up with even more tension later on. After a fair amount of time has passed, make an effort to get your child talking about the disagreement. Communicating and listening will ultimately open the doors to greater understanding.

Let them know that they are on your "most wanted" list. Say something like this: "If you feel as though you're on our 'most wanted' list, you're right! Regardless of all the conflicts we'll experience together, you really are wanted by us. We really do love you."

Before the Storm: Promote a Peaceful Environment

You're well aware that sibling rivalry is a fact of family life, yet few things can cause a parent to become a raving maniac quicker than constant bickering and fighting. So what's the answer? Is it possible to defuse the constant missiles your children launch at each other? Can you actually teach your children to be peacemakers? We think you can. While you'll never eliminate sibling rivalry, it is possible to improve your kids' attitude, foster mutual respect, and save your sanity.

Help them understand the conflict. Older kids and teens are very sensitive about personal injustice, self-worth, independence, privacy, and love. The next time they have a head-on collision with a sibling, encourage them to take three steps: (1) cool down, (2) identify the problem, and (3) talk it out.

Teach them to be problem-solvers. Help your child realize that when two people have trouble getting along, it's usually because a problem has built up over time. For example, if trust is the hot-button issue with a family member, he must get to the root of the problem. Say this: "Sit down with the one who wronged you, and figure out how to settle the conflict on your own. And as you confront your brother or sister, avoid assigning fault. Instead, concentrate on finding a solution to your problem."

Steer them away from sarcasm. Tell them: "One of the easiest ways to do battle is to make fun of your brother or sister, but it's also one of the most damaging. Cruel remarks have a tendency to hurt others deeply, and the wounds will keep on giving pain long after the issue has been settled."

Encourage them to show respect. Not only will family members return it, they'll also become less prone to quarreling. They'll even let them have their way from time to time.

After the Storm: Set Clear Boundaries

Help them avoid a "bitterness burn." Tell your child that "Bitterness hurts you far more than it hurts others. It's like a hot coal. The longer and tighter it is held, the deeper the burn. Bitterness can leave scars that even time cannot erase."

Encourage them to fight their own battles. Tell them: "Don't report every little disagreement to me. After you've cooled off, sit down with your brother or sister and figure out how to settle the conflict on your own. Concentrate on finding a solution to your problem without assigning blame."

Teach them to forgive—and then to forgive again. Tell them: "Think of all the ways you feel you have been wronged by your brother or sister. Then work toward genuine forgiveness. Understand that forgiveness is not denying that you've been hurt or even trying to understand why a person has acted a certain way. Genuine forgiveness involves consciously choosing to release the hurt someone has caused—and continuing to love that person. Can you get to that point with the family member who has wronged you?"

Clearing Up Parent–Kid Static with Older Kids

Conversation #1—How It Could Be...

Child: "I hate my English composition class, and I don't see the point in taking it. It's not like I'm gonna be a novelist someday."

Parent: "I hear you—writing can be hard. But, you know, I'm glad I stuck with it when I was your age. Is there any way I can help?"

Child: "I have to write a two-page theme paper tonight. Got any suggestions for a topic?"

Parent: "Have a seat, and let's see what we can dream up together."

Child: "Thanks. This really takes a load off my mind."

Conversation #2—How It Usually Is...

Child: "I hate my English composition class, and I don't see the point in taking it. It's not like I'm gonna be a novelist someday."

Parent: "I don't want to hear another complaint out of you. English is a requirement. Now get up to your room and do your homework."

Child: "You never listen to me when I have a problem. I can't wait till I'm on my own and don't have to put up with stupid rules."

Parent: "Keep it up, smart mouth, and you'll get yourself grounded."

Child: "This stinks. You are absolutely ruining my life."

Which conversation is typical with your older child or teen? Let us guess—the second one! Too bad, because Conversation #1 isn't that far out of reach. In fact, with some work, it can actually be the regular mode of conversation. But it all begins with an important nine-letter word: Listening.

"My parents just don't listen to me" is the anthem of many kids. Likewise, it's a complaint echoed by parents: "I can't get through to them—they just won't listen."

Listening is where effective communication really begins. Instead of engaging in a verbal tug-of-war with your child, follow these essential steps:

Begin with passive listening (or silence). Give your child a chance to speak his or her mind. "I'm just not getting anything out of playing soccer and really want to drop out. I can't keep up, and the coach always embarrasses me in front of everyone."

Give acknowledgment responses. Don't just stand there with a blank expression on your face. Even when you're listening passively, it's a good idea to make sincere comments, such as "I see" or "Oh?" that emphasize that you are paying attention.

Offer a "door opener." This is a simple, nonjudgmental statement, such as "How would you feel about talking to the coach after practice? Maybe she'll ease up on you." How-you-feel questions are less threatening to your child, and they help spark communication.

Exercise active listening with a communication style called "shared meaning." Here's how it works:

- You're frustrated because your child didn't clean his room before the dinner party, not to mention the mess he made on the patio. So you approach him and say, "We need to talk about this. I'd like you to hear my side."
- Once you have his attention, you explain your point of view (which you've thought through ahead of time) without being interrupted. Next, your child repeats what he heard you say.
- You then clarify or confirm what he said, ensuring that your thoughts and feelings have been heard accurately.
- The process continues with him sharing his point of view and you listening and repeating what he said.

The goal of shared meaning is to be heard accurately. And once you've had a chance to state your case and listen to his, the foundation is set for communication—and for a fair solution to the problem at hand—a solution that's grounded on listening and being heard ... not just another pointless Tuesday night fight.

AFTERWORD

Understanding, Loving...and Growing Together

Never let the idea that you have ADHD hold you back from reaching for your dreams or be an excuse on why you cannot get there.

—*Daniel G. Amen, M.D.*

Reading *Understanding and Loving Your Child with ADHD* has been the easiest step in your search for answers. Now comes the really hard part: putting into practice all that you've discovered within these pages. But rest assured—you're well on your way! Your child can experience a fresh start and a brighter future...and you both can secure a more peaceful home life. Here's what we've uncovered:

- A deeper understanding of your child's unique needs
- Practical ways to survive and thrive socially

- Better communication at school and on the home front
- A way to escape negativity and stress
- Tips to harness your child's creativity

As we've shown you throughout this book, ADHD is real, and it can be successfully treated. Yet it's imperative that we sort out the myths and stick to the facts.

Very often children with ADHD have at least one other mental, emotional, or behavioral disorder. Therefore, when doctors evaluate a child for ADHD, they must also look for other mental disorders that could be at play: depression, bipolar disorder, anxiety, obsessive-compulsive disorder, and tic disorders. Only by understanding everything that may be contributing to symptoms and addressing each of these issues can your child truly get well.

Your child can survive, and thrive, in spite of having to navigate ADHD. Concentration, alertness, and the ability to focus can be improved as you address his or her unique needs. This can lead to improvements in their problem-solving ability, productivity, and overall creativity.

Before we wrap up our conversation, let's recap some key facts about ADHD…

It's Time to See a Doctor If...

✓ There is a persistent pattern of inattention and/or hyperactivity-impulsivity

✓ Six or more of the symptoms have persisted for six months or longer

✓ Your child isn't developing socially or academically at a pace that's consistent with other kids his/her age

Just because a kid can't sit still or his or her grades are slipping doesn't mean ADHD is the culprit. The symptoms must be present every day for a long period of time and must lead to an impairment of a child's life for it to be true ADHD.

Common Behaviors Observed in Children with ADHD...

✓ They are constantly in motion

✓ They squirm and fidget

✓ They make careless mistakes

✓ They often lose things

✓ They often seem to tune out others and not listen

✓ They are easily distracted

✓ They often do not finish tasks

The essential feature of attention-deficit/hyperactivity disorder (ADHD) is a persistent pattern of inattention and/or hyperactivity-impulsivity that interferes with functioning or development.

Your Child's Health Will Improve and You Can Manage ADHD By...

✓ Paying attention to what they eat and drink
✓ Understanding that what children consume can have both a positive and a negative effect on their minds
✓ Achieving a sense of well-being and balance (homeostasis) with a holistic mind-body-emotions plan
✓ Allowing medical experts to prescribe the right medication for your child's unique needs

As we treat ADHD in children, we should implement a complete wellness program that includes proper diet, exercise, and supplements—all beginning with a physical and mental evaluation.

The ADHD Child May Exhibit...

✓ Out-of-the-box creative thinking
✓ A leaning toward sensation-seeking
✓ The ability to hyperfocus on subjects that interest
  them

With creativity, a "boundless attitude," and the desire to learn, we can think and create like some of history's greatest minds. Your child can, too!

In Social Settings, Children with ADHD...

✓ Are extremely poor monitors of their own social
  behavior and the reactions they provoke in others
✓ Don't know how to accurately assess or "read" a
  social situation
✓ Struggle when it comes to starting and maintaining a conversation
✓ Have a hard time finding acceptance among
  their peers

Your child can learn to read people better and improve relationships through (1) self-awareness, (2) self-management, (3) social awareness, (4) relationship management.

Daily Routines and Freeform Thinking Can Help the ADHD Child...

✓ Maintain a predictable environment
✓ Feel a sense of security
✓ Have the breathing room to engage their creativity

Every one of us can become a better version of ourself, including children with ADHD. Help your kid take steps in a positive new direction.

Your Relationship with Your ADHD Child Can Improve By...

✓ Having deeper empathy for them
✓ Intentionally building trust
✓ Finding ways to have consistent, balanced connections with them

Our relationships can improve as we improve trust, communication, and empathy with those we love and interact with.

As we said at the beginning of the book, our goal is to help parents like you learn how your children's minds work so you can connect with them in more meaningful ways—and ultimately help them improve their health, their relationships, and their overall quality of life.

Take heart—that kid of yours really is bursting with potential. The problem is that their distractibility and impulsivity (caused by ADHD) can put up roadblocks in their life. Without the proper spark from you, they could end up stuck in mediocrity—always dreaming, but never doing. It's up to you to fuel their imaginations. Get them excited about the future and all the possibilities ahead of them: the things they can experience, the places they can one day go…the very special people they are inside. Encourage them to dream big and to explore a few possibilities right now.

It's time to change their thinking…and transform their lives. Let's get going!

Notes

Chapter 1: Recognizing the Signs and Symptoms

1. What some public school administrators refer to as a "504 Plan" is a federal program offered by the U.S. Department of Education. Section 504 of the Rehabilitation Act of 1973 protects the rights of persons with handicaps in programs and activities that receive federal financial assistance. For more information, visit https://www2.ed.gov/about/offices/list/ocr/504faq.html.
2. American Psychiatric Association, *Diagnostic and Statistical Manual of Mental Disorders*, 5th ed. (Arlington, Virginia: American Psychiatric Association, 2013), 59.
3. Melinda Smith, Lawrence Robinson, and Jeanne Segal, "ADHD in Children," https://www.helpguide.org/articles/ADHD-adhd/attention-deficit-disorder-adhd-in-children.htm.
4. *Diagnostic and Statistical Manual of Mental Disorders*, 61.

5. "Attention-Deficit Hyperactivity Disorder (ADHD)," Harvard Health Publishing, Harvard Medical School, https://www.health.harvard.edu/a_to_z/attention-deficit-hyperactivity-disorder-adhd-a-to-z.

6. Smith, Robinson, and Segal, "ADHD in Children."

7. Professionals in the mental health field often refer to this guide as they diagnose psychological problems, including anxiety disorders.

8. "Attention-Deficit Hyperactivity Disorder (ADHD)," Harvard Health Publishing.

Chapter 2: ADHD Mythbusters

1. Edward M. Hallowell and John J. Ratey, *Driven to Distraction: Recognizing and Coping with Attention Deficit Disorder from Childhood through Adulthood*, rev. ed. (New York: Anchor, 1994), xiv.

2. Based on current data and statistics from the Centers for Disease Control and Prevention, U.S. Department of Health & Human Services, www.cdc.gov.

3. Harry Kimball, "Hyperfocus: The Flip Side of ADHD?," Child Mind Institute, http://www.childmind.org/en/posts/articles/2013-9-23-hyperfocus-flip-side-adhd.

4. See Daniel G. Amen, *Healing ADHD: The Breakthrough Program That Allows You to See and Heal the 7 Types of ADHD* (New York: Berkley, 2013).

5. Amen, *Healing ADHD*, xxxvi.

6. Ibid.

7. Ibid.

8. Gail Saltz, *The Power of Different: The Link between Disorder and Genius* (New York: Flatiron Books, 2017), 49–51.

9. Ibid., 57.

10. Amen, *Healing ADHD*, 84.

11. Saltz, *The Power of Different*, 58.

12. Ibid.

13. Jeffrey Zaslow, "What If Einstein Had Taken Ritalin? ADHD's
     Impact on Creativity," *Wall Street Journal*, February 3, 2005, https://
     www.wsj.com/articles/SB110738397416844127.

14. Ibid.

15. Ibid.

16. Amen, *Healing ADHD*, xviii.

17. Ibid.

18. See Smitha Bhandari, "ADHD Diet and Nutrition: Foods To Eat &
     Foods to Avoid," WebMD, June 27, 2019, https://www.webmd.com/
     add-adhd/adhd diets.

19. See "Stress: The Silent Killer," Holistic Online, ICBS Incorporated,
     http://www.holisticonline.com/stress/stress_diet.htm.

Chapter 3: Four Steps to Getting an Accurate Diagnosis

1.   Melinda Smith and Jeanne Segal, "ADHD Tests and Diagnosis," Help
     Guide website, September 2020, https://www.helpguide.org/articles/
     ADHD-adhd/diagnosing-attention-deficit-disorder-adhd.htm.

2.   Bob Seay, Laura Flynn McCarthy, and Penny Williams, "Your
     Complete ADHD Diagnosis and Testing Guide," ADDitude,
     September 13, 2019, https://www.additudemag.com/
     adhd-testing-diagnosis-guide.

3.   Laura Reynolds, "Teaching Children with ADHD: Classroom
     Strategies to Engage the Easily Distracted," Open Colleges, May 23,
     2013, https://www.opencolleges.edu.au/informed/features/
     teaching-children-with-adhd.

4.   "Symptoms and Diagnosis of ADHD," Centers for Disease Control
     and Prevention, https://www.cdc.gov/ncbddd/adhd/diagnosis.html.

5.   Ibid.

6.   Smitha Bhandari, "Attention Deficit Hyperactivity Disorder: Diagnosing ADHD," WebMD, June 11, 2019, https://www.webmd.com/add-adhd/childhood-adhd/diagnosing-adhd.

7.   Ibid.

8.   Laurel K. Leslie, "The Role of Primary Care Physicians in Attention Deficit Hyperactivity Disorder (ADHD)," National Center for Biotechnology Information, U.S. National Library of Medicine, PMC Journal, https://www.ncbi.nlm.nih.gov/pmc/articles/PMC1647398.

9.   National Institute of Mental Health.

10. American Psychiatric Association, *Diagnostic and Statistical Manual of Mental Disorders*.

11. C. Smith and L. Strick, *Learning Disabilities: A to Z* (New York: Free Press, 1997).

12. For an in-depth discussion, review our discussion in Chapter 1. Also, take a look at what the CDC has released. See this informative online article: "Symptoms and Diagnosis of ADHD," Centers for Disease Control and Prevention, https://www.cdc.gov/ncbddd/adhd/diagnosis.html.

13. Seay, McCarthy, and Williams, "Your Complete ADHD Diagnosis and Testing Guide."

14. Ibid.

15. Ibid.

16. "Attention-Deficit Hyperactivity Disorder (ADHD)—What Is It?" Harvard Health Publishing, Harvard Medical School, https://www.health.harvard.edu/a_to_z/attention-deficit-hyperactivity-disorder-adhd-a-to-z.

17. Seay, McCarthy, and Williams, "Your Complete ADHD Diagnosis and Testing Guide."

18. Ibid.

19. "FDA Permits Marketing of First Brain Wave Test to Help Assess Children and Teens for ADHD," Food and Drug Administration

news release, July 15, 2013, http//www.fda.gov/NewsEvents/
Newsroom/PressAnnounements/ucm360811.htm.

20. Elizabeth R. Sowell et al., "Cortical Abnormalities in Children and
    Adolescents with Attention-Deficit Hyperactivity Disorder," *The
    Lancet* 362, no. 9397 (November 22, 2003): 1699–707, doi:10.1016/
    S0140-6736(03)14842-8.

21. Daniel G. Amen, *Healing ADHD: The Breakthrough Program That
    Allows You to See and Heal the 7 Types of ADHD* (New York:
    Berkley, 2013), xiv–xv.

22. Seay, McCarthy, and Williams, "Your Complete ADHD Diagnosis
    and Testing Guide."

23. "Attention-Deficit Hyperactivity Disorder (ADHD)," Harvard Health
    Publishing.

24. Amen, *Healing ADHD*, xvi.

25. Sue McGreevey, "ADHD Linked to Substance Abuse Risk," *Harvard
    Gazette*, June 1, 2011, https://news.harvard.edu/gazette/story/2011/06/
    adhd-linked-to-substance-abuse-risk.

26. Amen, *Healing ADHD*, xiv–xv.

Chapter 4: Fearfully and Wonderfully Made

1. "Carol" and "Olivia" are pseudonyms. Their names were changed to
   protect their identities.

2. "What Is a Gene?" MedlinePlus, https://medlineplus.gov/genetics/
   understanding/basics/gene.

3. Gail Saltz, *The Power of Different: The Link between Disorder and
   Genius* (New York: Flatiron Books, 2017), 54.

4. Edward De Bono, *De Bono's Thinking Course* (New York: Facts on
   File, Inc., 1994), 1.

5. Ibid.

6. Barbara Wolff and Hananya Goodman, "The Legend of the Dull-Witted Child Who Grew Up to Be a Genius," http://www.albert-einstein.org/article_handicap.html.

7. Saltz, *The Power of Different,* 56.

8. Michael J. Gelb, *Discover Your Genius: How to Think Like History's Ten Most Revolutionary Minds* (New York: Delacorte Press, 1998).

9. Ibid.

10. Nancy C. Andreasen, "Secrets of the Creative Brain," *The Atlantic,* July/August 2014, https://www.theatlantic.com/magazine/archive/2014/07/secrets-of-the-creative-brain/372299.

11. Michael J. Gelb, *Discover Your Genius* (New York: HarperCollins, 2002), 318.

12. Ibid.

13. Dr. James Dobson, *Bringing Up Boys* (Wheaton, Illinois: Tyndale House Publishers, 2001), 4.

14. "Sensation Seeking," *Psychology Today,* https://www.psychologytoday.com/us/basics/sensation-seeking.

15. Darya L. Zabelina, David Cardon, and Mark Beeman, "Do Dimensional Psychotherapy Measures Relate to Creative Achievement or Divergent Thinking?" *Frontiers in Psychology* 5, no. 1029 (2014), doc:10.3389/fpsyg.2014.01029.

16. Gail Saltz, *The Power of Different,* 59.

17. Ibid.

18. Royce Flippin, "Hyperfocus: The ADHD Phenomenon of Intense Fixation," ADDitude, https://www.additudemag.com/understanding-adhdhyperfocus/#:~:text=What%20is%20ADHD%20Hyperfocus%3F,out%20the%20world%20around%20them.

19. Nanette Gingery, interview by Michael Ross, February 2014.

Chapter 5: Confidence Booster No. 1—Building Better Relationships

1. See the following article for additional ideas on how to handle bullying. Some of our tips were inspired by this website: ADDitude Editors, "In This House, We Don't Tolerate Bullying," ADDitude, https://www.additudemag.com/slideshows/no-more-bullying-strategies-for-adhd-kids.

2. B. Hoza, "Peer Functioning in Children with ADHD," *Ambulatory Pediatrics* 2007, no. 7: 101–6, doi:10.1016/j.ambp.2006.04.011.

3. Nora Bunford, Steven W. Evans, and Joshua M. Langberg, "Emotion Dysregulation Is Associated with Social Impairment among Young Adolescents with ADHD," *Journal of Attention Disorders* 22, no. 1 (2018): 66–82, doi:10.1177/1087054714527793.

4. Keath Low and Steven Gans, "How to Improve Social Skills in Children with ADHD," Verywell Mind, February 28, 2021, https://www.verywellmind.com/how-to-improve-social-skills-in-children-with-adhd-20727.

5. Denise M. Gardner and Alyson C. Gerdes, "A Review of Peer Relationships and Friendships in Youth with ADHD, *Journal of Attention Disorders* 19, no. 10 (2015): 844–55, doi:10.1177/1087054713501552.

6. Ibid.

7. Sarah Wilkes-Gillan et al., "A Randomised Controlled Trial of a Play-Based Intervention to Improve the Social Play Skills of Children with Attention Deficit Hyperactivity Disorder (ADHD)," PLoS ONE 11, no. 8 (2016), doi:10.1371/journal.pone.0160558.

8. Low and Gans, "How to Improve Social Skills in Children with ADHD."

9. Ibid.

10. Amori Yee Mikami, "The Importance of Social Contextual Factors in Peer Relationships of Children with ADHD," *Current Developmental*

Disorders Reports 2, no. 1 (2015): 30–37, doi:10.1007/s40474-014-0036-0.

11. Low and Gans, "How to Improve Social Skills in Children with ADHD."

12. Ibid.

Chapter 6: Confidence Booster No. 2—Balancing Structure with Spontaneity

1. Laura Reynolds, "Teaching Children with ADHD: Classroom Strategies to Engage the Easily Distracted," Open Colleges, May 23, 2013, https://www.opencolleges.edu.au/informed/features/teaching-children-with-adhd.

2. Keath Low, "Why Children with ADHD Need Structure and Routines," VeryWell Mind, November 8, 2020, https://www.verywellmind.com/why-is-structure-important-for-kids-with-adhd-20747.

3. Ibid.

4. Ann Dolin, "Stick to the Plan! How to Cement Your Child's New Home Learning Routines," ADDitude, https://www.additudemag.com/stick-to-the-plan-adhd-schedules.

5. Reynolds, "Teaching Children with ADHD."

Chapter 7: Confidence Booster No. 3—Harnessing Their Daydreams

1. Kate Kelly, "ADHD and Creativity: What You Need to Know," Understood, January 2021, https://www.understood.org/en/learning-thinking-differences/child-learning-disabilities/ADD-adhd/adhd-and-creativity-what-you-need-to-know.

2. Ibid.

3. Letitia Sweitzer, "How to Encourage Creativity in Children with ADHD," ADDitude, https://www.additudemag.com/positive-parenting-creativity-children-adhd-self-esteem.

4. "The Healing Power of Art," Harvard Health Publishing, Harvard Medical School, July 2017, https://www.health.harvard.edu/mental-health/the-healing-power-of-art.

5. Sweitzer, "How to Encourage Creativity in Children with ADHD."

6. Perri Klass, "Boredom: Could It Be Creativity's Spark—or a Cause for Concern?," Harvard Medicine, January 2021, https://hms.harvard.edu/magazine/adventure-issue/boredom.

7. Sweitzer, "How to Encourage Creativity in Children with ADHD."

8. Ibid.

9. Judy Arnall, "An Age-by-Age Guide to Nurturing Creativity in Kids," *Today's Parent*, November 16, 2020, https://www.todaysparent.com/family/parenting/an-age-by-age-guide-to-nurturing-creativity-in-kids/amp.

10. Ibid.

11. Ibid.

12. InternetWorld Stats, adapted from a June 30, 2009, web report, http://www.internetworldstats.com/stats2.htm.

Chapter 8: Confidence Booster No. 4—Launching a Better Tomorrow

1. Edward Hallowell, "12 Ways to Build Strong ADD Families," ADDitude, June 19, 2019, https://www.additudemag.com/12-ways-to-build-strong-add-families.

2. "ADHD Parenting Tips," Help Guide, https://www.helpguide.org/articles/-adhd/when-your-child-has-attention-deficit-disorder-adhd.htm.

3. Hallowell, "12 Ways to Build Strong ADD Families."

4. Ibid.

5. See this excellent article on this topic: Deborah Carpenter, "Never Punish a Child for Bad Behavior outside Their Control," ADDitude, https://www.additudemag.com/ behavior-punishment-parenting-child-with-adhd/.

6. Ibid.

7. Ibid.

8. Claire McCarthy, "The Better Way to Discipline Children," Harvard Health Publishing, Harvard Medical School, January 1, 2019, https:// www.health.harvard.edu/blog/ the-better-way-to-discipline-children-2019010115578.

9. Carpenter, "Never Punish a Child for Bad Behavior outside Their Control."

10. McCarthy, "The Better Way to Discipline Children."

11. Claire McCarthy, "Resilience: A Skill Your Child Really Needs to Learn (and What You Can Do to Help)," Harvard Health Publishing, Harvard Medical School, updated August 16, 2020, https://www. health.harvard.edu/blog/ resilience-a-skill-your-child-really-needs-to-learn-and-what-you-can-do-to-help-2017061311899.

12. Ibid.

13. "This Evidence-Based Approach Improves Student Behavior and Engagement," Education and Behavior, January 18, 2021, https:// educationandbehavior.com/ how-to-help-students-with-behavior-problems.

14. McCarthy, "The Better Way to Discipline Children."

15. Ibid.

16. Deborah Carpenter, "Never Punish a Child for Bad Behavior outside Their Control," ADDitude, September 19, 2019, https://www. additudemag.com/behavior-punishment-parenting-child-with-adhd.